ELECTRIC DREAMS

DESIGNING
FOR THE
DIGITAL
AGE

**DAVID
REDHEAD**

V&A
PUBLICATIONS

To my mother and father

First published by
V&A Publications,
2004
V&A Publications
160 Brompton Road
London SW3 1HW

ISBN 1 85177 409 2

V&A Publications
160 Brompton Road
London SW3 1HW
www.vam.ac.uk

A catalogue record for
this book is available from
the British Library

Design and cover
photography by
Graphic Thought Facility

Printed in Italy

ELECTRIC DREAMS

DESIGNING FOR THE DIGITAL AGE

AUTHOR BIOGRAPHY

David Redhead is the editor of 'Grand Designs' magazine. He began his career in design at the multi-disciplinary design consultancy Fitch in the 1980s, before making his name as a writer and design critic. A contributing editor to 'Blueprint', former editor of 'Design' magazine, managing editor of 'Blueprint' and columnist for 'Design Week', he has also written for newspapers and magazines including the 'Guardian', 'Independent', 'Independent on Sunday', 'Sunday Times', 'Daily Telegraph', 'Sunday Telegraph' and 'The Financial Times'. He is the author of 'Products of our Time' (August/Birkhauser, 1999) and 'The Power of 10: ten products by ten British product designers' (Laurence King, 2001).

ACKNOWLEDGEMENTS

I am grateful to the many designers and manufacturers who talked to me at length during the preparation of this book, and to all those featured who supplied images and other essential information. I would also like to thank the following people for their help in making **ELECTRIC DREAMS** possible: Jane Pavitt; Mary Butler and her team at V&A Publications; Eunjoo Maing and Paula Kovacs for additional research; Krystyna Mayer for editing the text; Graphic Thought Facility for the design; Melanie and Michael Andersen and Simon Horton for their hospitality during my research trip to California; and my wife Sara for her constant patience and support.

SERIES FOREWORD

Design is an essential component of everyday life, in ways that are both apparent and imperceptible. But who are the authors of the things that surround us? What drives the thinking behind the development of new products? Designers leave their imprint on these products in a diversity of ways, through projects ranging from cutting-edge experimentation to the restyling of mass-market goods. They shape the objects with which we furnish our homes, the tools with which we communicate and the environments in which we live, work and play.

The V&A Contemporary series explores the designer's role in shaping products of all kinds – from the one-off to the mass-produced, from objects created in three dimensions to digital environments. The series celebrates modern creativity and diversity in design, highlighting key debates and practices, and confronting us with questions about the future of our designed world. Each title takes a critical and informed look at a particular field, built around interviews with designers and commentaries on selected products and projects. We hope these studies encourage us all – designers and consumers alike – to look with fresh insight at the objects and images around us.

Jane Pavitt, Series Editor

AUTHOR'S FOREWORD

ELECTRIC DREAMS: DESIGNING FOR THE DIGITAL AGE explores the changing shape of what used to be called 'consumer electronics' products over the past twenty years. It is not, of course, a comprehensive history. Such is the pace of innovation that you would need a volume a hundred or a thousand times bigger to analyse every trend in the field. Rather, the book presents a snapshot of an electronics world in mid-revolution. It examines how product designers are increasingly shaping technology to our needs and desires, and reflects on what these changes tell us about the evolving shape of twenty-first-century digital consumerism.

ELECTRIC DREAMS charts the seismic shifts that transformed the monochrome product world of 1980s electronics into a volatile modern landscape full of shape, colour and variety. It considers the economic and technological imperatives that brought design to the heart of electronic innovation and marketing culture. It reveals how the complexity of modern technology has added a new social and anthropological dimension to the creation of mini-disks and microwave ovens, radios and robots.

To add detail and depth to the story, separate chapters have been devoted to three digital product types that define the millennial zeitgeist. **ELECTRIC DREAMS** dissects Apple's output from the iMac to the iPod to show how digital manufacturing's ultimate paradigm-shifter made us learn to love the computer. It analyses the combination of boffinish entrepreneurial flair and sleek styling that allowed the Personal Digital Assistant (PDA) to cross the chasm to consumer success. And it introduces the designers who turned brick-like mobile phones into miniature symbols of 'fashion-tech'.

ELECTRONIC CONSUMERISM COMES OF AGE

'ONCE DESIGN WAS ABOUT DESIGNING OBJECTS. NOW IT'S ABOUT ANTICIPATING BEHAVIOURS. DESIGNERS NEED TO BE FILM DIRECTORS RATHER THAN SCULPTORS.'

TIM BROWN, IDEO

It is a measure of how familiar techno-consumerism has already become in the third millennium that the **RADIO IN A BAG** designed by Daniel Weil in 1981 has lost a good deal of the shock value it once had. Twenty-one years after the designer conceived it, it is perfectly feasible to imagine an updated version of this colourfully packaged transistor on sale as a novelty item in your local electrical store, alongside retro offerings from Bush or a youth-focused digital radio released under the Ministry of Sound brand.

You can certainly guarantee that, if it were to be relaunched in a slick updated package, the arrival of the Radio in a Bag on the shelves of the design stores would be marked by little of the controversy that surrounded Weil's output of radios when he first began production of his limited editions (manufactured in Tokyo by Apex from 1983). The Argentinian-born, UK-based designer had some influential supporters back in the mid-1980s, including the authors of 'New British Design', a survey of cutting-edge graphics, products, and architecture.[1] The book immediately hailed its sister product, the **THREE WAY RADIO**, as a vibrant icon of the brave new age of technology, using it as the book's cover image. Other critics found it wilfully obscure.

CALCULATOR
Sinclair Radionics Ltd.
UK
1991
V&A:M.17–1991

In a lecture on 'the Englishness of English design' professional zeitgeist-watcher Peter York wrote off the Three Way Radio as a 'lopsided mousetrap'. 'They call it design but you can tell from the price that it's actually art,' he wrote. 'Now the compilers of 'New British Design' think that this is an important little radio. They think it's a milestone in British design. They put it on the cover. My instinct is to step on it…' [2]

One can forgive York his sense of incomprehension, if not his blimpishness. Daniel Weil's aim was to anticipate what the electronics of the near future might look and feel like, but the very notion of deconstructing a radio and repackaging it must have been hard to fathom in the early 1980s. Today we are all techno-veterans, but then the digital age had yet to make any impact on our everyday lives. The first Apple Mac was still two years from the market, the first laptops and commercial mobile phones five years distant and the Personal Digital Assistant (PDA) wouldn't even find itself a name for another decade. Back then, consumer electronic products for home entertainment were known prosaically – and a bit inaccurately – as brown goods. Meanwhile, fridges, cookers, washing machines and the like were 'white goods', and at that time they almost always lived up to the banal description.

RADIO IN A BAG
Transistor radio components in a printed PVC bag
Daniel Weil, manufactured by Apex, Japan,
designed in 1981, manufactured in 1983.
V&A:W.9–1992

JELLY PHONE, XK200 TWINPHONE
Swatch (Switzerland)
manufactured in Taiwan
1990
V&A:W.3–1996

←—
MOBILE TELEPHONE
Soft Series products
Emilio Ambasz & Associates, Inc., USA
1990

↓
MINISTRY OF SOUND DAB
(Digital Audio Broadcasting) Radio
Therefore Product Design for Ministry of
Sound Audio, UK
2003

PROSSIMO TELEPHONE
(prototype), designed by Tadao Amano, Italy
1992–3

Of course, there were colourful and exciting electronic products made in the late 1980s (Swatch watches and the Sony Walkman immediately spring to mind) but despite these flashes of technological and marketing genius, a lingering Fordism continued to retain its grip on the electronics mainstream until the early 1990s. 'Brown goods were very sterile,' says Stefano Marzano, Design Director at Philips. 'Many had all the consumer appeal and character you expect of an old-fashioned medical appliance.'

A survey of a few consumer electronic products that featured in design magazines in the early 1990s reveals the accuracy of Marzano's view. Granted, there were always manufacturers such as Bang & Olufsen for whom design was essential, and there was some experimentalism going on at the margins, such as Tadao Amano's splendidly futuristic **PROSSIMO TELEPHONE** (1993). Some influential avant-gardists like New York-based Emilio Ambasz and big-name designers like Philippe Starck even found manufacturers to make their products. Yet on the whole, cutting-edge technology rarely seemed to be treated to adventurous styling. The grey rectilinearity of the new PDA Sony launched in 1992 was a good deal closer to the norm than Ambasz's adventurous new collection of soft devices for the Italian company Brionvega (1993) or Starck's gloriously eccentric moulded TV for French company SABA (manufactured by Thomson, 1994).

THE SUPERMARKET OF STYLE: FROM RETRO TO MINIMAL

Bearing in mind the conservatism of the 1980s and early 1990s, it is extraordinary to observe how attitudes have changed in the following decade or so. 'Brown goods' still lingers on as a title of convenience for the entertainment electronics sector, but many products have discovered all the joys of 'lifestyle' branding. They are certainly subject to the same segmentation that applies elsewhere in the 'supermarket of style' that is modern product design. As for so-called white goods, in the late 1980s Zanussi's black fridge with a red flag on the top was a rare postmodern novelty (part of the The Wizards Collection, designed by Roberto Pezzetta in 1987). Now fridges and cookers in every pastel shade and every metallic finish are par for the course.

Visit any product-design studio with an interest in consumer electronics today and you will find consultants ready and willing to offer phones, radios and TVs in colours or flavours pitched at every sort of taste and age range. Manufacturers cultivate the youth market with stylistic variations ranging from rugged urban (Motorola's **TALKABOUT TWO-WAY RADIO**) to the sci-fi sinister (almost any gaming handset). Older audiences are courted with new kinds of products in forms that, like the **APPLE iPOD** or Samsung's concept for a **LOFT LIVING TV**, are in line with minimal trends in furniture and fashion, or whose sporty styling matches their function (as in the case of Nike triax sportswatches).

←
TALKABOUT TWO-WAY RADIO
model T5820, manufactured by Motorola
2002

↓
ANALOG JOYSTICK GAME PAD
STAR TREK MOUSE
Smart Design, LLC
manufactured by VM Labs, USA
1996

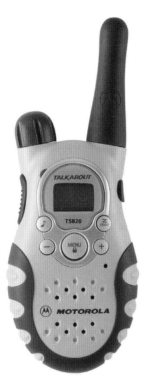

**TYPHOON WATCHES AND WATER SPORTS
TIMING DEVICE**
Pentagram, manufactured by Nike, USA
1998

↓
EVOKE-1 DAB RADIO
Pure Digital
(Imagination Technologies), UK
2002

Arguably the biggest growth area has been in retro styling, perhaps because its appeal seems to span the age gap. Manufacturers such as Bush have re-editioned classic radios or commissioned modern redesigns of mid-twentieth-century designs – an example is the new Bush retro modern radio designed in 2002 by British product designers Therefore. Nor are manufacturers diffident about combining nostalgic design with new technology. Pure Digital's **EVOKE-1 DAB RADIO**, far and away the most popular model on the nascent British digital radio market, is presented like a slick throwback to the 1960s, and James Irvine's microwave concept for Whirlpool also has a retro-modern feel.

So why have product designers who spent so long on the sidelines found themselves suddenly thrust to the centre of the development process? Stefano Marzano, appointed Design Director at Philips in 1992, has since presided over a nearly four-fold growth in his Eindhoven-based team, from 120 in 1992 to 460 in 2003. Marzano believes that at first, the new emphasis on design reflected the humanistic spirit of the zeitgeist. 'Following the end of the Cold War, a new ethical dimension took root that made us all think about the values of the things that surrounded us,' he says.

↓
RETRO RADIO
Therefore Design, manufactured by Alba
China
2003

↘
SOUNDWAVE ELECTRONICS
microwave oven with an electric door and
integrated FM radio (design concept)
James Irvine, for Whirlpool
the Netherlands
2000

In the assorted manifestos Marzano produced at the time, he proposed a 'New Modernity' that would bring to products 'quality rather than quantity…and simplicity rather than complexity'. 'It was about creating a new paradigm. The idea was to use our technology to create a new quality of life for consumers,' Marzano explains. 'It was vital that we built warmer, more meaningful relationships with electronics than the cold, hard-edged products of the 1980s had.'

Perhaps. But while the dreamy idealism of the so-called 'caring, sharing 1990s' had a hand in it, the design boom undoubtedly was more about pragmatism than idealism. Like many other electronics manufacturers, Philips had endured a sales slump with the global recession of the early 1990s. Design was already the word on the lips of many commentators – the influential American magazine 'Business Week' predicted at the start of the 1990s that design would be 'the corporate buzzword of the decade'. [3] It was a natural step, then, that established manufacturers desperate for new ways to bolster the appeal of their brands should give product designers their chance.

HOT BADGE 'ICE BREAKING' SHORT RANGE COMMUNICATOR

(design concept)
Vision of the Future Project, Philips,
the Netherlands
1995

LUDIC ROBOTS

(design concept)
Vision of the Future Project, Philips,
the Netherlands
1995

NEW WALLET WITH SUPER SMART CARD

(design concept)
Vision of the Future Project, Philips,
the Netherlands
1995

SKI JACKET WITH PERSONAL NAVIGATOR

clip-on camera/microphone/earpiece
(design concept)
Vision of the Future Project, Philips,
the Netherlands
1995

FUTURE FORECASTING: PHILIPS AND AMBIENT INTELLIGENCE

Product design was coming to be viewed as a necessity rather than a luxury by the global consumer electronics establishment, but its accession to a new position of power was rarely easy. For example, the investment in and expansion of the design team at Philips took place against the context of cuts and radical reshaping elsewhere in the organization. 'Philips was trying to restructure and to revitalize at the same time,' recalls Stefano Marzano. 'But it was a difficult policy that was not well understood in the company at first.'

The key to Marzano's success in winning over the Philips' sceptics was, he believes, the success of an experimental project which he used to test the market for electronic products with more personality. Soon after he acceded to the position of Philips' Design Director, Marzano contacted Alberto Alessi, whose designer homeware company was itself already experimenting with more accessible and cheaper collections of domestic objects.

Alessi quickly agreed to Marzano's proposal for a collaboratively produced collection of small domestic appliances. These drew on Alessi's creative resources – making use of the avant-garde designer Alessandro Mendini as Creative Director – and used Philips' manufacturing expertise. 'At the time, Philips' coffee-maker team only made coffee makers and nothing else,' explains Marzano. 'The Alessi project was more cross cultural and it provided the catalyst for a product proposition that was more poetical, more emotional.'

Launched in 1994, the resulting collection of whimsical-looking, pastel-shaded kettles, toasters and coffee-makers proved popular enough with the public to win Marzano the support of Philips' Chairman, J.D. Timmer, for an ambitious forecasting programme. The company initiated 'Visions of the Future', a comprehensive review of Philips' entire product portfolio which set out to anticipate how each product area would develop in the following ten years. The exhibition and book that followed in 1996 envisaged a utopian landscape populated by a cuddly-looking and colourful new breed of digital devices.[4] Among these are the **SHIVA PDA**, **HOT BADGES** that signal to each other when their wearers have something in common, **VIDEOPHONE WATCHES**, **LUDIC ROBOTS**, a ski jacket incorporating a personal navigator, and a wallet reminiscent of Emilio Ambasz's early 1990s' soft concepts.

RANGE OF DOMESTIC PRODUCTS
Alessandro Mendini
manufactured by Alessi/Philips,
Italy
1994

The momentum of Philips' design initiatives has not slowed since. Indeed, the speculation has gathered momentum. Today, Philips anticipates a shift towards a connected world in which all the objects that surround us will have the potential to communicate with each other, a phenomenon that Marzano and his team have christened 'ambient intelligence'. In this digital landscape, designers will of necessity have a much broader role. As a recent press release puts it: 'According to our vision, design is far more than the skill that makes products attractive, practical, convenient and marketable. With the development of complex Ambient Intelligent solutions design will play a key role. Not only will it shape the way objects will look, feel and be used, but it will also define how they will behave and interact with people through time'.[5]

Philips is not, of course, the only company to have reached this conclusion. Different manufacturers have their own different names for ambient intelligence (Canon has called it Ubiquitious Computing, for instance). But whatever it is called, this vision of a connected world has informed almost all of Philips' future-forecasting exhibitions and other initiatives that have followed. These include Connected Wheels, a collaboration on a digital and sustainable concept vehicle with Renault in 1997, The Home of the Near Future in 1999, New Nomads, an exploration of wearable electronics in 2000 and, most recently, Philips' collaboration with the Italian company Cappellini on concepts for 'ambient intelligent' furniture at the Salone dei Mobile in Milan in April 2003, which included the **VESUVIO** sofa-cum-ceiling-projected-TV.

Stefano Marzano estimates that 95 per cent of the Visions concepts are now on the marketplace. And while only 5 per cent of these are made by the Dutch company, Marzano insists that the new design process has contributed directly to the bottom line. 'It's led to our claiming the position of global leader in small domestic appliances,' he says.

VESUVIO
ceiling projector/circular sofa, part of the
Paesaggi Fluidi Project (Flowing Landscapes)
Stefano Marzano and Guilio Cappellini,
manufactured by Philips/Cappellini, Italy/
the Netherlands
2003

COMPETITION IN THE EAST:
SAMSUNG INVESTS IN DESIGN

Philips' self-conscious drive to present itself as an agenda setter in digital design has made it the most visible of manufacturers to have thrown its weight behind innovation and design. But other less-vaunted companies have been following a similar path. Samsung is a case in point. Until six years ago, the giant Korean company was by its own account a second-rate brand that relied on me-too or copy-cat products and low prices to compete. That all changed in 1997, when Samsung's Chairman, Kun Hee Lee, committed the company to a design-driven new-product-development policy that would challenge Toshiba, Sanyo, NEC, Sharp and, above all, Sony on its own upmarket territory.

Samsung decided to move upmarket because things had started to look crowded at the bottom. New electronics manufacturers were already springing up in China and the so-called 'tiger' economies of east Asia. The cheap output of these interlopers was threatening to undercut the profit margins not only of the established electronics manufacturers like Philips, but also of the 'second-tier' manufacturers like Samsung. 'The company decided it had got as far as it could purely on price,' says Mark Delaney, Design Manager of the company's twelve-strong London studio. 'The management decided that the company had the technology and production capability to compete for consumers by making products that were really well designed and a pleasure to use.'

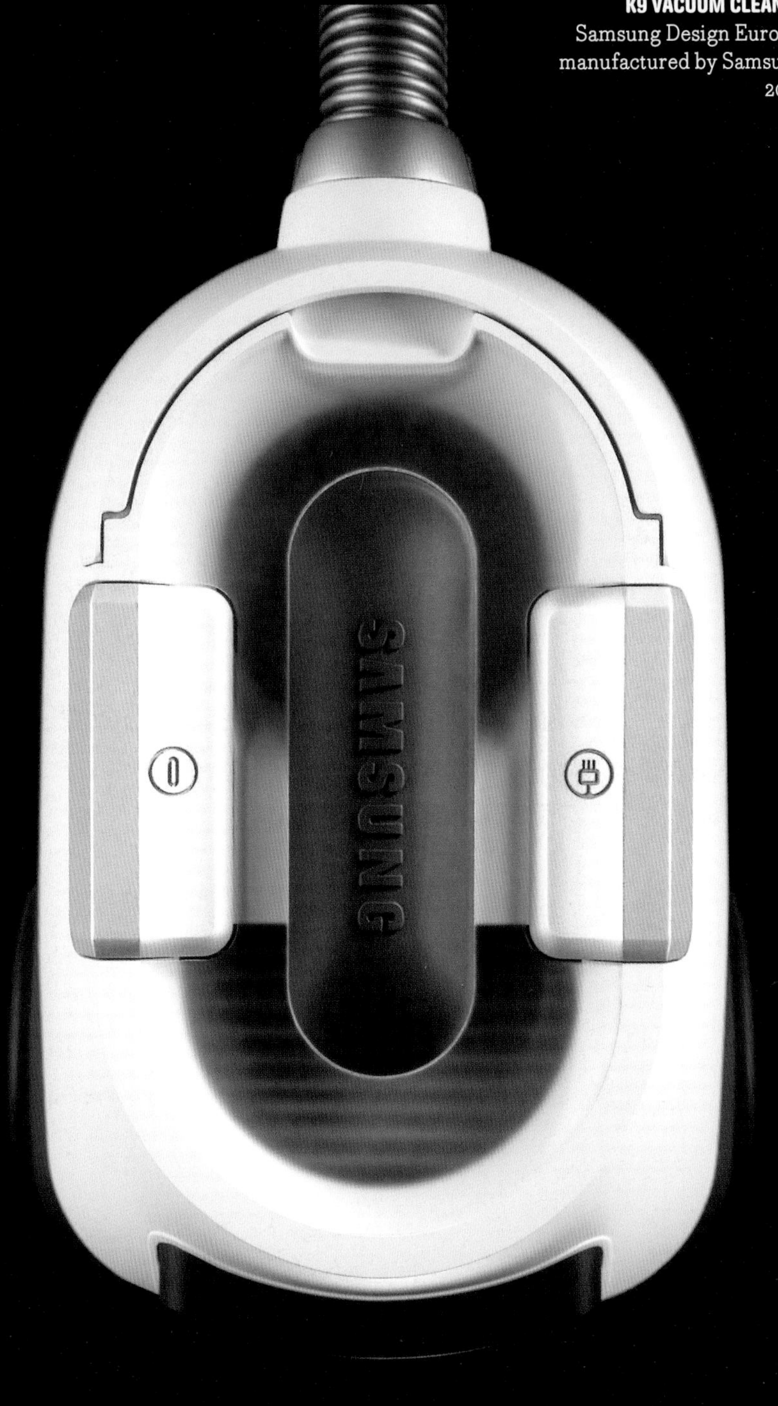

K9 VACUUM CLEANER
Samsung Design Europe,
manufactured by Samsung
2002

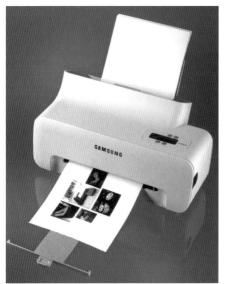

PRINTER
(design concept)
Samsung Design Europe, UK
2000

→
ALUMINIUM AND RUBBER MICROWAVE
(design concept)
Samsung Design Europe, UK
2001

Following Chairman Lee's initiative, Samsung set up its own design academy for 200 students in Seoul, simultaneously establishing satellite design studios in Japan, the UK and California in the US. It also brought in consultants Gordon Bruce and Tom Hardy from the US – Bruce to set up the school and Hardy to help answer the central questions that the whole exercise begged. What exactly was Samsung design? How should it be turned into a product and what should that product look and feel like? 'We needed both a visual identity for Samsung products and a tool for evolving design concepts into products,' says Mark Delaney. 'Eventually we established a language that was about "simplicity with resonance" – simplicity with an emotional factor – which could apply to a mobile phone or a big television.'

The project stalled in 1998 as Samsung struggled to cope with the slump in east and south-east Asia, but the programme quickly revived and gathered pace when Samsung began to bounce back in the early years of this decade. Since the year 2000, the Seoul design school has grown to 300 students, and satellite design offices have been re-established in London, San Francisco and Tokyo, each with its own particular responsibility for honing an aspect of the Samsung brand.

The London studio run by Mark Delaney has proposed over forty concept projects for the consideration of the Seoul design headquarters, among them a vacuum-cleaner 'with the basic character of a mop and bucket', a microwave oven 'with the sub-industrial character of a Dualit toaster', a home appliance totem for space-saving urbanites and a mysteriously retro-modern printer. 'The Californian office's expertise is more strategy and user-interface focused while our team is more about honing the Samsung design language,' explains Mark Delaney. 'Often their taste in Seoul is for design with a noisier character, products which celebrate technology. Our role is to try to challenge that way of thinking and to drag them back to something that is simpler and more understated.'

Delaney admits that Samsung covets a 'future seed'– a product like Sony's cuddly, playful robots, which constitutes an attention-grabbing public relations vehicle that confirms its status as a ground-breaker and innovator. But its design initiative is already having an impact on the image of the Korean company. Samsung has found a design flagship, if not a future seed. The flip-top **V200** mobile phone (see p.117) designed by Samsung's team in Seoul is currently not only the biggest selling mobile phone in China, but is also viewed as one of the trendiest designs on the European market.

SONY 'AIBO' LATTE AND MACARON, ERS 311 ROBOTS
manufactured by Sony, Japan
2001

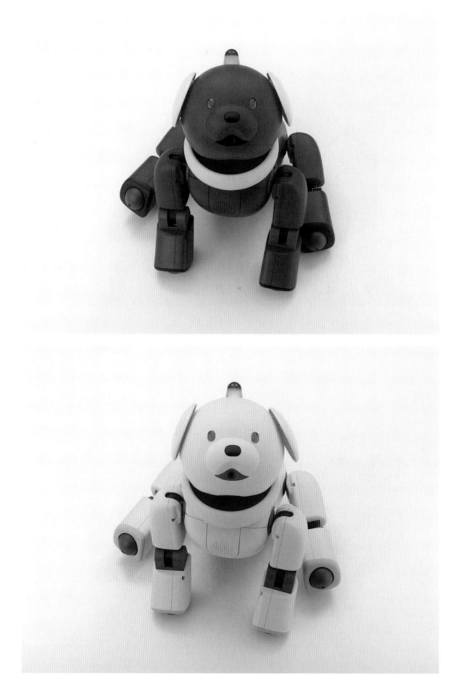

FROM USEFUL TOOLS TO DESIRABLE OBJECTS: SILICON VALLEY STYLE

FLAT PANEL DISPLAY & SIMPLE PC CONCEPT STUDY
(design concept)
Robert Brunner and Pentagram,
for Hewlett Packard, USA
2002

The entertainment end of the consumer electronics market was where most of the action took place as the design bandwagon gathered pace in the early 1990s. At that time new digital products that were only beginning to find their feet in the real world, such as laptops and mobile phones, still often had the downbeat air of technical tools. But as the case studies in this book illustrate, product design has played a growing part as competition has hotted up in these markets since the mid-1990s. The mobile phone, for example, has become a fully fledged consumer object with models targeted at different users and age groups.

The Anglo-American product-design specialist IDEO has been especially well placed to observe the transition of new-wave digital products from useful tools to desirable objects. The company's design studio in Palo Alto, California has been deeply involved with many of the Silicon Valley techno-entrepreneurs who have been at the cutting edge of product development. IDEO played a significant role in the makeover that transformed the **PALM PILOT** from what one of its designers called an 'object for geeks' into the fashion-conscious and unisex **PALM V**. The Palm Pilot has sparked imitators, such as the **COMPAQ iPAQ** and variations like the **EXECUTIVE PDA** concept by New York-based digital design specialist Antenna.

ENJOY INKJET PRINTER
(design concept)
Robert Brunner and Pentagram
for Hewlett Packard, USA
2002

↓

ACCOMPLISH NOTEBOOK
(design concept)
Robert Brunner and Pentagram
for Hewlett Packard, USA
2002

This development pattern – you might call it the 'ugly duckling syndrome' – has become typical for techno-innovation. At first the boffin-cum-entrepreneur (such as Palm's Jeff Hawkins or Psion's David Potter) launches the clever but ugly gizmo, then the competition kicks in and the original innovator turns to design to stay ahead. IDEO's UK Director, Colin Burns, cites Geoffrey Moore's book 'Crossing the Chasm' as a key influence on IDEO's new-product-development philosophy. 'Moore understood that the key moment is when you stop selling on technical performance and start marketing on the basis of life scenarios,' says Burns. 'That's when an electronic product has the ability to 'cross the chasm' from being an object for early adopters to becoming a consumer product.' [6]

PALM V
Designed by IDEO
manufactured by Palm, USA
2000

EXECUTIVE PDA
Design concept
Designed by Antenna Design for Palm,
USA
2000

It's also hard to underestimate the impact of the first **APPLE iMAC** in shifting attitudes to design at the business end of electronics manufacturing. Since the iMac succeeded in 'crossing the chasm' so spectacularly in 1998, design has begun to reach parts of the industry that were once unknown territory. Hewlett Packard is a typical example. The company has usually been viewed as a technology-savvy maker of printers and other business-focused machines that paid little attention to visual consistency. But in 2001, the company set about unifying its brand image, its advertising and its marketing programme under the motto 'Invent'. Hewlett Packard commissioned design consultancy Pentagram to devise a flexible product-identity programme that would give its wide range of products more coherence and more consumer appeal. Even Microsoft, which is often seen, rightly or wrongly, as the last refuge of the beige computer, is waking up to design.

Bill Sharpe, Director of the specialist Bristol-based product-development consultancy Appliance Design and himself a former Hewlett Packard employee, sees parallels between this shift in electronics and the sudden rush of design development that revolutionized the form of cars in the middle of the twentieth century. 'As a technology becomes abundant and people begin to take its reliability for granted they also start to think about how the product fits with their self image,' he argues. 'As a result manufacturers have to start competing with products that are not just functional but appropriate and delightful too.'

IN SEARCH
OF EMERGENT
BEHAVIOURS:
DESIGNERS AS
ANTHROPOLOGISTS

You can only drive the automotive parallel so far. It's one thing giving your ranges a visual makeover, but designing for the millennial digital world is likely to prove a good deal trickier than it might have been for the pioneers of mid-twentieth-century car design. There are certainly many more variables to consider. At least Harley Earl, the man behind General Motors 1950s' extravagances, knew that almost everything he designed was likely to have four wheels and an internal combustion engine.

By contrast, the product designers of the digital era often seem to be designing a moving target. How exactly will 'Ambient Intelligence', as conceived by Philips, translate into successful products on the shelves of the electrical shops? Will the sort of connected products that are already making their way onto the consumer electronics market, like LG Electronics' Internet-connected fridge or Sharp's microwave oven, take off? What form will the mobile phone take in five years? Will the PDA – already a highly volatile item – even survive that long?

The product-design waters have been further muddied by the financial uncertainty that surrounds communication technology. That processor power will continue to increase is not in doubt, but what is less clear is how manufacturers and network providers will make money out of it. In the mid-1990s, companies such as Vodafone were prepared to bid billions of dollars for the licensing rights to so-called 3G mobile technology. It is clear now that they are unlikely to recoup those investments in a hurry, if at all.

Richard Seymour, a founding partner of the London-based product-design consultancy Seymour Powell, believes that everyone involved in new-product development will have to learn to take these new uncertainties in their stride. He compares the current dilemma facing those in the digital communication, manufacturing and service industries to that encountered by the turn-of-the-twentieth-century pioneers after another revolutionary discovery: that of electricity. Seymour maintains that the network providers who overbid so heavily for their stake in 3G technology did so because they missed the point: 'They mistook the digital "hows" for the "its". It's not the technology that matters but what people are able to do with it,' he maintains.

Seymour argues that in considering the future development of products for the digital age, investors, designers and manufacturers would do well to learn from the mindset of a great modern inventor of the age of electricity, Thomas Edison. 'Edison knew that we didn't really care how electricity worked. His genius was in understanding that technology only became profitable when you found applications for it that changed people's lives,' Seymour argues. 'His concern was not with the "hows" of the technology but the "its" – the light bulb, for example.'

Seymour Powell's decision to supplement its teams of designers, engineers and model-makers with a dedicated team of future forecasters is driven by this increasing need for designers who can make sense of the digital shifts taking place. 'Designers today need an anthropological streak,' says Seymour. 'They need to anticipate the emergent behaviours that new technologies will make people capable of and how they will choose to use them.'

Irene McWilliam, Professor of Computer Related Design at the Royal College of Art, and until recently Director of Design Research at Philips, believes many of the leading manufacturers have already followed the Dutch manufacturer in adding this anthropological strand to their design teams. They have supplemented the traditional contingent of engineers, designers and marketers with researchers, technologists and social scientists who are ever-more expert at forecasting, developing and making products as specialist fashion accessories, business tools or entertainment devices.

**EXPERT CHEF INTERACTIVE
LEARNING TOOL**
Vision of the Future Project,
Philips, the Netherlands
1995

'Social science and product design is a highly effective combination,' McWilliam argues. 'It adds a reflective and challenging dimension to design but it also generates products that feel real and which become a real tool for looking at the future as well as a catalyst for future developments. Envisaging a product gives you a starting point for debate and discussion. It makes forecasting more powerful and valid.'

The many uncertainties and complexities that are clouding a clear vision of the digital future are also forcing product-design consultants in the electronics field to rethink their skills. 'When I started out, product design was about designing objects,' says Tim Brown, CEO of IDEO. 'Now it's about anticipating behaviours. What that means is that you won't be able just to attach design to the product. In the future, designers will need the skills of movie directors rather than those of sculptors.'

And it seems they will need the skills of entrepreneurs to boot. The designer of the Psion organizer, British product-design consultancy Therefore, was viewed as something of an electronics specialist when it set up in business in the early 1990s. But in the past five years it has found work in the sector less and less easy to come by. 'There are very few manufacturers in this country with their own factories who would use us as consultants in the traditional sense,' says Therefore Director Graham Brett.

As well as looking further afield for clients, Therefore is trying to develop more of its own product ideas for the marketplace. In 2003, it was planning to launch the **PHONEBOOK**, a new mobile phone by the Chinese company Inventec Appliances. This business-focused design draws indirectly on the company's 'personal organizer' experience, incorporating a full-size fold-out keyboard designed by Martin Riddiford that Psion would have been proud of (see p.99).

OUTSIDE THE GHETTO: THE MISSING COUNTER CULTURE

The development of multi-disciplinary electronic teams may have made for consultants who are quicker on their feet, in-house designers who are better informed and products that are more sophisticated. But it is questionable whether the objects they have created are any more beautiful. Indeed, electronic products with a simplicity, distinctiveness, attention to detail, connectivity and coherence to compare to Apple's recent output are distinctly thin on the ground.

Designers from outside the electronics 'ghetto' such as the furniture and product designer Marc Newson have serious doubts about the design of electronic products. 'Music and a mobile phone are necessities for me,' says the Australian designer. 'But if I didn't have to buy electronic products I wouldn't bother.' Newson's background is primarily as a furniture designer, but he has also created watches, bicycles and a distinctly striking concept car for Ford, the 021C. He argues that electronic-product design 'is full of the gratuitous stylistic clichés' that have recently defined the world of automotive design. 'Products look so artificial, so nurby, as if they have been designed on screen rather than in three dimensions,' he says.

Newson's criticisms find support among a number of electronic design insiders. Sam Hecht now runs Industrial Facility, his own consultancy, but as a senior designer with IDEO for several years, Hecht is a veteran of the territory. 'There are good manufacturers who understand how to use design to reinforce their brand and their position in the marketplace – Sony, Bang & Olufsen, Loewe, Apple, for instance,' says Hecht. 'But on the whole the standard of design is dismal.'

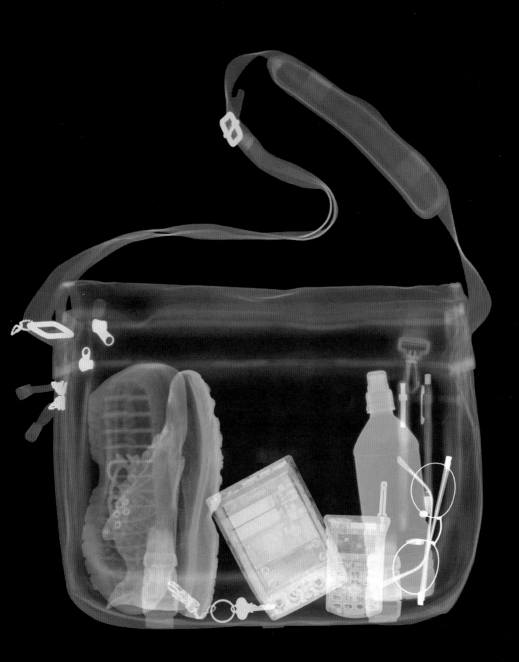

→

RE-SP – Bootleg Objects
(MP3 server playing smart chips on 1980s Technics DJ turntable)
Max Wolf, Markus Bader and Sebastian Oschatz in Germany,
manufactured by Droog Design, the Netherlands
2003

Perhaps the shortage of real classics has something to do with the ab-
sence of an individualistic counter-culture in electronic-product design.
The British designers Anthony Dunne and Fiona Raby are one of only a
handful of avant-garde groups to have made a living from designing electronic objects outside the mainstream. 'Students do come up with ideas
but the expense involved in the development process means that the
prototypes pretend to do something rather than actually doing it so the
ideas stay in the realm of fiction,' says Tony Dunne. 'If designers are
going to experiment they usually have to join a manufacturer like Philips
or a design consultancy like IDEO.'

There are exceptions to this rule. In 2003, German designers Max Wolf
and Markus Bader made a telling comment on this homogeneity in the
form of three working limited edition designs called **BOOTLEG OBJECTS** for the
Dutch company Droog. All three are updates of established classics: the
BRAUN AUDIO 1 radio/record player designed by Dieter Rams in 1962, the **BEO-
CENTER 7700 'MUSIC CENTRE'** from the 1970s and the **TECHNICS SL 1210**, the classic
'scratching' dance turntable of the 1980s. Each object looks much as it
always has but has been modified so that it makes use of modern digital
technology. The **REBRAUN AUDIO 1**, for example, plays MP3 files and runs off
Microsoft Windows 2000.

As Max Wolf sees it, the objects draw on a 'ready-made' design tradition to make a wry comment on both the quality of electronic design and the notion of interface. 'Rebraun is a homage to Dieter Rams although it mocks the rationalistic tradition of design a little by adding features such as a "Random" button in a random position,' he explains. 'But it is also a comment on how boring consumer electronics design is. I don't think you could really say that the aesthetics of electronic design has moved on much since Rams designed the Audio 1.'

Perhaps the truth is that individualism does not often sit well with the well-oiled marketing machine that is consumer electronics. The Milan-based English product and furniture designer James Irvine is in a good position to judge. He spent a year working for Toshiba in the late 1970s and has kept a toe in electronics, recently designing the elegant **EB15** fax machine for Canon. In his view the two product-design worlds are largely alien to each other. 'The nature of big manufacturing design studios is that they are democratic places in which everyone gets their say. I have sat in many meetings within large organizations where a marketing manager says "the buttons must be elliptical because that's what the bestselling things have today"' he explains. 'But the best design is not created by a democratic process. It is forced through by powerful and talented individuals.'

RE-BO – Bootleg Objects
(memory card reader, touch screen, wireless speakers, headphones
in chassis of 1973 Bang & Olufsen Beocenter Hi-Fi system)
Max Wolf, Markus Bader and Sebastian Oschatz in Germany,
manufactured by Droog Design, the Netherlands
2003

REBRAUN – Bootleg Objects
(PC-based MP3 player, FM Radio, Internet
streaming radio in chassis of 1962 Braun Audio 1 system)
Max Wolf, Markus Bader and Sebastian Oschatz in Germany,
manufactured by Droog Design, the Netherlands
2003

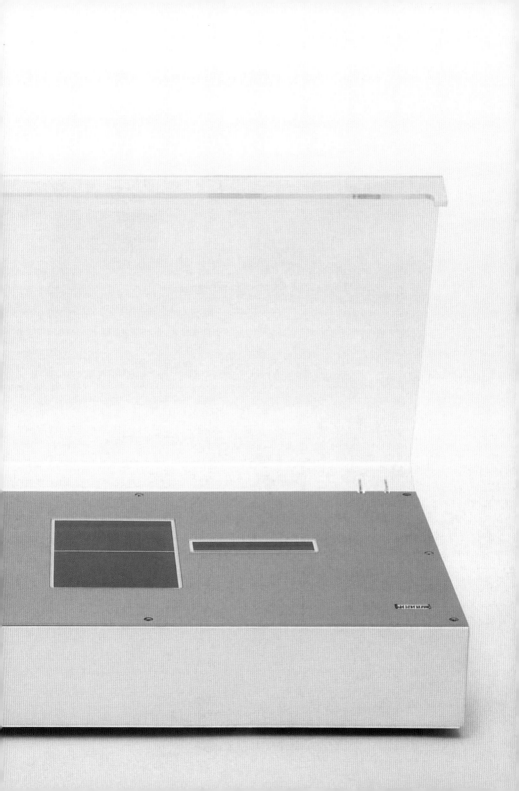

NEW ELECTRONIC BRANDS:
THE RISE OF RETAILER POWER

Individualism may yet become a stronger ingredient in electronic design, however, thanks to shifts in the economics of manufacturing. Britain is not the only country to be running short of electronics manufacturers of its own. With the cost of labour in the West so high, even companies like Apple are sub-contracting the manufacture of their products to factories in the Far East. Cannier retailers are taking advantage of this shift to wrest control of product design away from the manufacturing names. In the US, the budget retailer Target has launched its own-brand collections of domestic digital objects by 'trophy' designers such as Philippe Starck, sub-contracting Black & Decker to manage the manufacturing process. Postmodern designer Michael Graves has been the popular success in Target's collection, with products ranging from colour printers, through cordless phones to stereo speakers.

Sam Hecht is convinced that more and more retailers will be taking a leaf out of Target's book. 'It's increasingly the retailers who are calling the shots by telling the manufacturers "this is what our customers want. Make it for us,"' he claims. He argues that, despite all their efforts to claim the design and innovation high ground, shifts in economics continue to threaten the weaker manufacturers. Says Hecht, 'I think a lot of manufacturers have a tough battle on their hands. Imagine if Walmart, the world's biggest corporation, starts commissioning its own electronic products.'

The increasing number of retailers who are investing in their own electronic products are indeed giving all but the strongest of manufacturers pause for thought. Hecht himself has been at the vanguard, creating an elegant phone for the 'no-brand' Japanese retailer Muji, as part of a new collection of electronic products to which his former IDEO colleague Naoto Fukasawa has also contributed.

BGM
3

1. Pastorale siciliana
2. Tarantella napoletana
3. Il carnevale di Venezia
4. U sciccareddu jbamento
5. Gran valzer
6. Contradanza
7. Mi votu e mi rivotu, vieni, vieni
8. La traviata -Preludio all'atto 1
9. Tarentina - si beddu tu
10. Torna a Surriento
11. Passeggiando per Lipari
12. Mi vutu e mi rivotu
13. Cavalleria rusticana -Intermezzo
14. Vitti 'na crozza

MUJI
無印良品

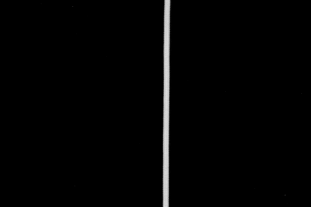

PRADA LOYALTY CARD
Sam Hecht/IDEO for Prada
2002
Photograph by Lee Funnell/Domus

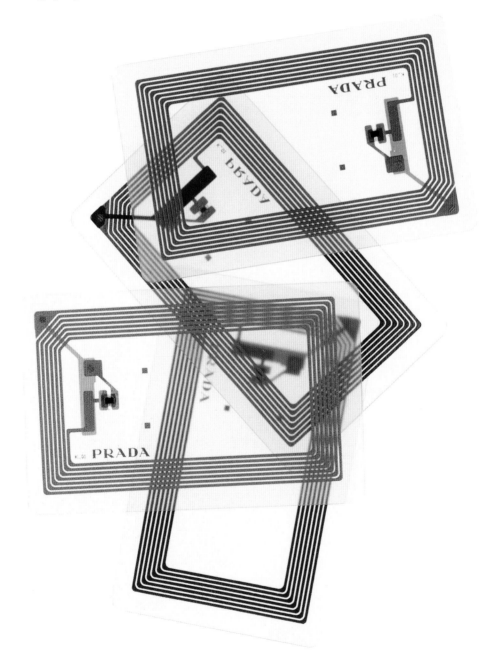

STAFF DEVICE
Sam Hecht/IDEO for Prada
2002
Photograph by Lee Funnell/Domus

Perhaps the most influential of Hecht's high-profile electronic-product-branding projects so far has been his work for the fashion label Prada, undertaken during his time at IDEO. Conceived as part of the flagship New York store created by the fashionable architect Rem Koolhaas, the electronic-design programme was integral to a $30 million investment intended to ramp up Prada's profile to new and more fashionable heights. Designed to 'allow Prada staff to choreograph in-store sales experiences for customers', the focal point of the programme is a customized **iPAQ PDA** housed in Prada-branded transparent skin which 'navigates local and global information systems with a clinical efficiency that is sympathetic to the design ethic of Prada itself'.

DRINKS ORDERING SYSTEM
Sam Hecht and Durrell Bushop/IDEO
for Orange/Manumission,
manufactured by IDEO, UK
2002
Photograph by Lee Funnell

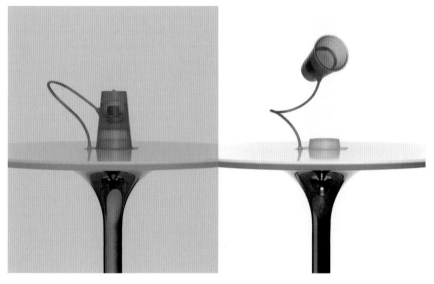

The PDA in turn connects to customer loyalty cards in the form of Prada-branded circuit boards. In essence, these are all stock-checking and customer-record tools, but the impact of the programme on the Prada brand clearly goes much deeper than tracking the whereabouts of items of clothing. Banks of the recharging PDAs feature as strong design elements in the interior of the shop, for example. 'A company like Prada wants unique things that project its authority in its field,' says Hecht. 'They wanted a PDA and a loyalty card that was in line with their own design philosophy. What better way is there of projecting their leadership than giving them ownership of the circuit board?' Nor is the shift confined to retailers. In his time at IDEO, Hecht worked with Durrell Bushop on the design of a drinks-ordering system co-sponsored by Orange for the Ibiza club Manumission. The Ministry of Sound, a club and music label, has also commissioned a new collection of own-brand electronic products from designers Therefore.

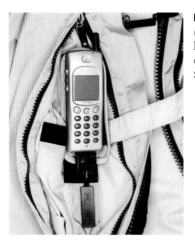

LEVI'S ICD +
(wearable technology)
Massimo Osti, for Levi's/Philips
collaboration, UK
2000

IL TELEFONO ALESSI
Stefano Giovannoni, manufactured
by Alessi/Siemens, Italy
2003

It is striking, then, that some of the most original ideas and the more individual consumer-electronics designs are emerging from retailers, service providers and entertainment brands. It is a trend that has not escaped the notice of more enlightened manufacturers. Philips has worked with Levi's on wearable technology and Siemens recently entered into a collaboration with Alessi that has already generated a new cordless phone for the home designed by Italian designer Stefano Giovannoni (**IL TELEFONO ALESSI**, 2003).

TELEPHONE
Sam Hecht/Industrial
Facility for Muji, Japan
2003
Photograph by Ryohin Keikaku Co., Ltd

Uli Skrypalle, Design Director of the German company's mobile product division, views this decision to go with the flow as a pragmatic response to the twists and turns of a volatile market and the strengths and weaknesses of his own brand. He is, he admits, receptive to the notion of both collaborating with other brands and using designers from beyond the electronic ghetto. 'Siemens has a great name for engineering and innovation but when it comes to a fashionable image we need help,' he says. Skrypalle says his mind is open to design perspectives from all sorts of designers from outside electronics, as well as to collaborations 'with fashion companies or sports brands depending on the functional and image requirements of the customer... There are no limits to the branding possibilities.'

TALBY PHONE
(back view)
Marc Newson, manufactured by KDDI,
Japan
2003

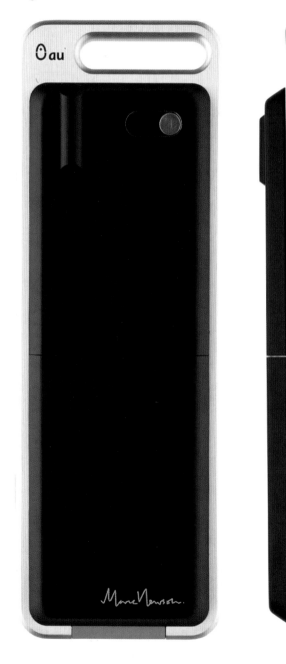

This open-minded view of electronic-product design is gaining currency, if the experience of Jasper Morrison is anything to go by. Morrison may be the leading British furniture and product designer of his generation, but he has had a couple of false starts in electronics. In 1998 he was asked to design a top-of-the-range video, hi-fi and TV 'with a furniture aspect', working alongside Sony's then in-house designer John Tree. But though the project threw up strikingly different prototypes the ideas were never put into production. Two years later, in 2000, Morrison joined Marc Newson in creating a camera concept for Canon. But the two designers' stripped-back vision of the camera was greeted with bewilderment by the Japanese company. 'They were totally baffled by what we did,' says Morrison. 'They couldn't understand that it didn't have a "styling concept" or that it wasn't some sort of exercise in nostalgia.'

Now the electronic world may be ready to embrace Morrison. His studio bolstered by the recruitment of John Tree, Morrison is reported to be creating a new-product collection for the appliance manufacturer Rowenta. Marc Newson may also be about to break through. His new ultra-simple phone for KDDI, Japan's leading mobile phone brand, is scheduled for launch in 2004. 'The time is ripe for more electronic products from independent designers,' says Newson. 'It's just bound to happen.'

It remains to be seen, of course, how many of these ideas will take off. Yet their very existence as 'real projects' illustrates how much attitudes to manufacturing, design and branding in consumer electronics have been transformed. Back in the age of the black box, the idea of putting a radio in a plastic bag was enough to provoke bemusement. Today we find nothing shocking or odd about the notion of a fashion-branded mobile phone, a customer loyalty card for a clothing store in the form of a circuit board or a radio 'produced' by a dance-club label. Indeed, in a few years' time they'll probably look as old-fashioned as a 1980s' brick mobile.

62–81

HOW APPLE MADE US LEARN TO LOVE THE COMPUTER

'APPLE IS THE ULTIMATE EXAMPLE OF A COMPANY THAT MAKES TECHNOLOGICAL OBJECTS DESIRABLE.'

TIM BROWN, IDEO

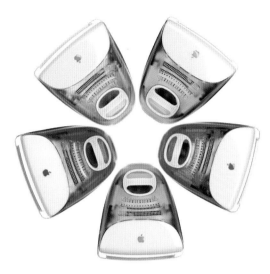

iMAC
Jonathan Ive and
Apple Design Team,
manufactured by Apple
Computing Inc.,
USA
1998

If designers, technologists and business people were all asked to name one company, one product and one designer that have most influenced attitudes to consumer electronics innovation since 1990, I'm confident that Apple, the iMac and Jonathan Ive, respectively, would feature strongly on all three lists. Industrial designers, especially those employed 'in house' by manufacturing corporations, do not often make the headlines but, since he signalled his talents with the sensational launch of the **iMAC** in 1998, the Newcastle-Polytechnic-educated British designer has emerged as the most influential product designer since Raymond Loewy. Today Ive's sphere of influence has moved beyond product design to encompass the fashion, business and popular culture mainstream.

In the past two or three years Ive and the iMac have been lionized – along with most of his other creations, bestselling and otherwise – in a cross-section of opinion-forming magazines, from design 'cheerleaders' like 'Wallpaper', through style-making and fashion titles like 'The Face' and 'Vogue', to business and current affairs media like 'The Financial Times' and 'Time'. Ive has even been labelled a 'genius' by 'Time', which featured him at number forty-four on a list of the world's most significant technology movers and shakers.[7] His importance has been recognized by professional bodies from the British Royal Society of Arts, who awarded him their inaugural medal for design achievement in 1999, to London's Design Museum, which named him Designer of the Year in 2003.

It's not hard to see why Ive has found the spotlight. He has played a leading part in a comeback story implausible – and irresistible – enough to serve as a good plot for a Hollywood buddy movie. A maverick business leader (Steve Jobs) returns prodigal-like as CEO of the once-successful corporation he founded that has now fallen on hard times. He strikes up a partnership with the quiet but inspired head of design (Jonathan Ive). Together the pair embark on a creative crusade, a product revolution that shatters the dull certainties that were once seen as the IT industry's immutable truisms: successful computers are about processor power; they are beige; one good product cannot save a company.

Ive also remains the designers' designer partly, you suspect, because of his low-key approach to his craft. Apple's products may be instantly recognizable, but Ive is a fierce critic of designer egoists and, unlike his only rival for the title of world's best-known (non-fashion) designer, the flamboyant Frenchman Philippe Starck, he is neither a showman nor a creator of 'shapist' trophies. Yet the products he and his largely anonymous team have created have an unusually wide resonance for different audiences: entrepreneurs, designers, technologists, trendspotters and, above all, the people who buy them.

APPLE IN DECLINE: THE EARLY 1990S

When I first met Jonathan Ive in London in 1996, the possibility of his emerging as a significant figure seemed remote. Ive had joined Apple in 1992, when the company's reputation for innovation and maverick character already set it apart from its rivals in the impersonal, corporate world of high technology. Founded in Palo Alto (the heartland of Silicon Valley, California) in 1976 by marketer Steve Jobs and technologist Steve Wozniak, Apple Computer had challenged the conformism of the personal computing business with its user-friendly approach to product development. It had found success with the **APPLE II**, **III** and later the **APPLE MAC** (designed by US consultancy Frogdesign and launched in 1984).

Ive's decision to join the company in house had been sparked by the desire to empower himself by 'getting closer to the place where decisions are made'. Like many product specialists he had become frustrated by his inability to get his ideas made as he conceived them or to connect with the board-level executives who made real strategic decisions.

His hunch didn't seem to have paid off, though. By the mid-1990s the innovation culture that had thrown up Apple's 1980s' classics seemed a thing of the past. Turnover had peaked at £12 million in 1995 and Apple was on the slippery slope. By 1996 the **NEWTON**, Apple's courageous but decidedly unpocket-sized PDA (designed by Thomas Meyerhoffer, a member of Ive's team) had flopped. Design Director Bob Brunner had left to join the design consultancy Pentagram and chief executives were coming and going with alarming regularity. There were a few pearls among the banal computers Apple was shipping – in 1996 the company launched the **eMATE**, a laptop in eye-catchingly colourful translucent polycarbonate pitched at school-children – but overall the outlook was bleak.

eMATE
Thomas Meyerhoffer and Apple
design team, manufactured by
Apple Computing Inc., USA
1996.
Winner of the 1997 D&AD
Silver Award for most outstanding
product for work.
Picture courtesy of British Design
& Art Direction.

iBOOK
Jonathan Ive and Apple Design Team,
manufactured by Apple
Computing Inc., USA
2000

Instead of finding himself closer to the reins of power, Ive felt sidelined within a company that in his own words appeared to be 'drifting towards oblivion'. 'Back then we had the same design team as today,' Ive told me in 1998. 'Yet we were totally useless…We were shipping some tedious bland products that spoke volumes about the company's lack of self-identity. We were obsessed with focus groups and research – in itself a symptom of a terrified company that won't develop anything of consequence.'

Many influential business commentators seemed to agree. Some were already penning the obituaries of a company that Ive admitted was 'rudderless'. As Jim Carlton of the 'Wall Street Journal' wrote at the time: 'this brave but foolhardy pioneer of the information age had experienced a plunge so rapid that it is tantamount to a snowball picking up speed and size as it hurtles down the mountain. Can anyone stop it or slow it down? Maybe, but it doesn't look good.' [8]

APPLE BITES BACK:
THE iMAC

Remarkably, Ive was about to be asked – to extend Carlton's metaphor – not just to slow down the snowball but to ski uphill. The designer could reasonably have suspected that he might lose his job when Steve Jobs returned to the company he had founded as interim CEO in 1997, twelve years after his boardroom ousting. But while Jobs fired most of the creative agencies then retained by Apple he clearly saw the potential of the product-design department. Ive's team of ten found themselves with the instant access to the boardroom they had always craved. 'We began working on the **iMAC** the day that Steve returned to the company,' Ive recalled in 1998. [9]

Jobs' brief was to design a consumer computer that would reclaim the spirit of the original 1980s' machines and dovetail this quality with a new strand of Web consciousness. 'We wanted to create an object which people felt they could dominate rather than the other way around. It was driven by a human set of priorities that I think the original Macintosh team would have shared,' Ive told me later.

With Jobs under pressure to signal his return by getting a new product onto the market, most of Apple's critics expected the first product to be more a stopgap than a comeback. According to mid-1990s' IT orthodoxy, after all, progress in computer design and manufacture meant simply more processor power and speed. Everyone knew that if Jobs were to improve on Apple's much-admired and copied user interface it was bound to take time. Yet when the new computer was launched in August 1998, a year after Jobs' return, it demolished industry expectations.

The iMac sold 150,000 units on the weekend that it was launched, sparking a feeding frenzy. One of the leading American computer warehouse chains sold more iMacs on one day in August than all the PCs it had shifted in the previous month. Before long, Apple's plummeting share values were also enjoying a bounce, climbing by 400 per cent over the following year and putting a stop at least temporarily to rumours of the company's imminent demise.

iMAC
Jonathan Ive and
Apple Design Team,
manufactured by
Apple Computing Inc.,
USA
1998

So what was it about the iMac that the public found so irresistible? After all, while the machine offered a tidy email, Internet and PC package in a value-for-money £800 deal, some critics found the lack of new technology disappointing: 'It doesn't provide a unique or new experience beyond the box,' Gitta Salomon, the Principal of interface design specialist Swim, wrote in a review for 'Design' in 1998. [10] Ah yes, but what a box it was! The iMac's ubiquity over the past six years has made it hard to recall just how extraordinary it looked to us at the time. Ive had wrapped Apple's hardware within the coloured polycarbonate skin he had experimented with on the eMate to create a cool and curvaceous translucent computer that looked like no other. Beside it, the bland boxes that constituted the competition suddenly looked like yesterday's technology.

In one sense the new look signalled Apple's return to its roots – back in the heady 1980s, the company's advertising and design had always emphasized its credentials as the human alternative to the Microsoft monolith. Its friendly lower-case logo (so different from the hard-edged, hi-tech authority of IBM) had a simplicity that seemed to suggest computing could be child's play. The iMac was the first step in re-establishing the distinction that had faded since Jobs' departure a decade before for the new age of home computing. But it also tapped into a fashionable lode that Apple's computers had not explored the first time around. This new incarnation of Apple values was not just domestic and different, it was also desirable.

TIME MAGAZINE
(14 January 2002,
'Flat-out Cool!'
and 26 June 2000,
'The Rebirth of Design')

Consumer conscious-
ness of interior style, architecture and product design had been growing
throughout the 1990s and the iMac was perfectly timed to surf the new
lifestyle wave. Thanks to companies such as the German accessory
manufacturer Authentics, which commissioned designers like Konstantin
Grcic to design all sorts of household objects in the material, translucent
plastic was already the furnishing flavour of the moment in Europe. By
bringing similar sleek lines and trendy colours to the computer, Apple
made the iMac a fashion statement. Here at last was a machine making an
unashamed pitch to a buyer whose priorities were, as the advertising put
it, 'chic not geek'.

Detail was everything. Ive and his team even consulted sweet manufacturers to ensure that the clear plastic casing looked as good on the
inside as it did on the outside. 'People focused on the translucency because
it was so immediate, but everything about the iMac was so different,' Ive
told me in 1998. 'Every little detail was considered, from internal structure
and fixings down to the product labels that are three-dimensional and
appear to move. We had to design the inside as well as the exterior.'

But there was more to the iMac's appeal than its 'come-hither' styling. The
independent spirit that its form implied was also very much in tune with the
zeitgeist. This was a work tool that stood apart from the daily grind of a
nine-to-five job. At a time when many younger consumers were already
growing cynical about corporatism, Apple's idiosyncrasy seemed to set it
apart from other global brands. For some, buying into the iMac's colours
and curves even seemed like striking a blow for individualism against the
massed forces of homogeneity. As an article in 'The Face' put it in 2002, 'If
Microsoft is the evil Empire then Apple is the Rebel Alliance and Jobs is
Obi-Wan Kenobi, Yoda and Luke Skywalker rolled into one'. [11]

INNOVATION FALLOUT: APPLE'S INFLUENCE

Now established as an icon of alternative and lifestyle culture, the iMac began to make waves in the business community too. In the early 1990s few corporations in the IT sector had seen design innovation as a way forward, but in the years that followed that began to change. American business gurus like Tom Peters and Gary Hamel were becoming increasingly influential in promoting an innovation agenda. Hamel's influential book 'Competing for the Future' (co-authored with C.K. Prahalad), published in 1994, argued that businesses must pursue a policy of continuous strategic innovation, aggressively seeking and building new markets.

As the Internet boom fanned the spark of innovation culture into a flame, Apple stood out as a role model for this innovation theory, the arrival of the iMac apparently crystallizing its strands into a single attractive product. The innovation fallout was most visible in the Californian techno-hothouse that is Silicon Valley. Suddenly funds became available for new products like PDAs and Web browsers that capitalized on these emergent new markets. Soon the shock waves were being felt all over the US.

Even stodgy PC manufacturers started waking up to the possibilities of design, according to design consultant Gitta Salomon. 'Suddenly everyone was coming to us and asking if we could help them create an iMac,' she recalls. As 'Time' magazine acknowledged in its cover story about design two years later, the iMac 'inspired a raft of whimsically styled low-cost personal computers from firms like Dell, Gateway and Compaq'. [12]

2–HANDS
Laundry basket
Polypropylene. Konstantin Grcic
Industrial Design for Authentics GmbH,
Germany
1996

SDC-80 (N.E.X.C.A.) camera
manufactured by Samsung
2001

Perhaps the most predictable spin-off of the iMac's success was the 'candy plastic' craze. Soon every other telephone, television and PDA that followed in the next year featured a translucent – and often tacky – cover or case. Yet the copy-cat culture didn't bruise Apple. 'Most of the products in translucent plastic only served to emphasize how outstanding the iMac was,' says Gitta Salomon. 'There was such rigour in its tooling that everything else looked like a shoddy rip-off.'

Coming up with one world-beating product is no guarantee of continuing prosperity in a market as relentlessly demanding as IT, of course. Other hardware manufacturers, such as Psion and Handspring (both innovators in the field of PDAs), have experienced financial difficulties despite their early product successes. The launch of the iMac, however, has proved less of an end in itself than the end of the beginning. 'What's astonishing about Apple is that in a market in which so many products look out of date or ugly they didn't just create one outstanding product,' says Ive's friend, Australian product designer Marc Newson. 'They keep on reinventing themselves and it's always stuff that I want to own.'

Reinvention – or at least radical reshaping of products on a continual basis – has become the mantra of strategy specialists such as Gary Hamel during the last ten years. It has certainly been the name of the game for Apple over the past seven. By the time its competitors were getting the hang of candy-coloured translucent plastic, Apple had moved on. In the years since the launch of the first iMac, Ive has moved on to embrace a new, somehow more sophisticated language with products ranging from the 'which-way-is-up' form of the **G4** hard drive to the four-square minimalism of the **CUBE** that followed in 1999 and 2000.

A BRAND IN DETAIL: FROM G4 TO NEW iMAC

Ive remains passionate about pushing the boundaries of his craft and retaining the perspective of a designer rather than a businessman. 'I have always been fascinated in how you make and build things and in new ways of using and building with materials,' he says. 'Something like a new way of bending a tube can create a whole new product language.'

This passion for experimentation was the quality that shone out from the retrospective of Ive's work for the Design Museum's Designer of the Year exhibition in 2003, with much of Ive's analysis of his product portfolio reading a bit like an enthusiastic technical manual. 'The primary approach was to maintain all the features within the overall product silhouette,' he wrote about the 12" PowerBook G4. 'The hinge details, bottom and catches are co-planar with the primary surface.' [13]

Some view Ive's preoccupation with new production processes and materials as a bit fetishistic, but the distinctive forms make sense from a branding viewpoint – the curving plastic skin that encloses the G4, and now also the **G5** box, is clearly uncopiable. Ive himself has always been eager to emphasize that his designs were driven more by the desire to 'make technology accessible and less scary' than merely by the wish to stand out from the crowd. 'You need to understand that our goal wasn't differentiation but to create products that people would love,' he has said. 'Differentiation was a consequence, not an end in itself.'

POWER MAC G5 TOWER
Jonathan Ive and Apple Design team,
manufactured by Apple
Computing Inc., USA
2003

iBOOK
Jonathan Ive and Apple Design
Team, manufactured by
Apple Computing Inc.,
USA
2001

If you examine Apple's recent products closely you can grasp how this concern for user and product experience translates into the details. Among the designer's own favourites are the mouse whose 'click' can be adjusted so that it suits the weight of your hand, and the bar codes that have been etched, instead of stuck as labels, on the underside of the new iMac. Then there is the 'breathing' sleep indicator on the G4 which pulses on and off as if it's gently snoozing: 'We are completely fanatical about every little detail,' Ive explains. 'Everyone else has a sleep monitor that just flashes on and off. But solving the functional imperative is not enough. We wanted something that seemed to be an organic breathing thing.' [14]

Of the **iBOOK**, Apple's self-contained laptop computer, Ive says: 'The iBook was designed for both the consumer and education markets. A continued concern for durability prompted us to combine polycarbonate shells with a die-cast internal frame. Critical components such as the hard drive were shockmounted.

Elements susceptible to damage such as the doors, external buttons and latches were eliminated as we developed the idea of the entire product being hermetically sealed by its external surfaces. The white colour coating was applied to the internal surfaces of the transparent plastic. Even the sleep-state LED monitor does not penetrate the external surface and only becomes visible when the unit is asleep as it gently cycles from dim to bright . . .'

There seems little doubt that this sort of attention to detail has helped to add to Apple's fan base in the past few years. Today the company's devotees have come to expect solutions that are daring. The launch of the new iMac with its radical detached screen may have been greeted by 'Business Week' magazine as illustrating the company's 'gradual slide into irrelevance', but the public voted with its collective mouse. The new iMac has beaten both analysts' earning predictions and revenue targets.

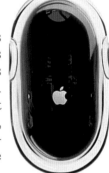

It is relatively easy to identify what has made Apple's products outstanding over the past few years, but it is becoming far more difficult to pin down what it is about the design process that makes it work so well. Today the company is almost neurotically reticent about its design policies. It won't show models, drawings or sketches. Meanwhile Ive works a seventy-hour week and is considered a virtual recluse by the Silicon Valley design community.

What is clear, however, is that Steve Jobs' relationship with Ive is growing in importance year by year. Jobs has a reputation for poor man-management skills. One former employee has described the atmosphere in the corridors, workshops and studios of Apple's Cupertino headquarters as 'poisonous and political'. If this is true, the design team seems to be sheltered from the bitchiness and backstabbing.

Jobs is not generally known for his willingness to give his employees the credit they deserve, but the easy-going and unflappable Ive is a big exception. According to one report, Ive and his team were given a whole extra year to come up with a new design for iMac 2 when the first concept failed to live up to expectations. And when 'Time' ran an exclusive piece about the launch of the new iMac in 2002 (see p.70), Ive was given equal billing in the pictures and described in the copy as 'Gilbert to Job's Sullivan'.[15] Ive returns this loyalty with his own, describing Jobs as 'an extraordinary designer in his own right'.

CONNECTED FUTURES: FROM iTUNES TO iPOD

It's hard to avoid the feeling that, perhaps even more than in the company's early days, the success and survival of Apple rests on the continuing harmony of a highly productive creative partnership. The company's recent product output does not suggest that there is any danger of the well drying up just yet. The convergence of computing and communication has allowed the creation of a new wave of digital products that cater for a new set of social and personal behaviours – from Web browsing to downloading and playing music. And Apple has already proved it can create portable products that make the most of this opportunity, as well as continuing to tap into the emotional aspects of the product-user relationship.

The **iPOD** is a case in point. An MP3 player launched in 2001–2 with an elegant circle-within-a-square simplicity, the iPod connects to both PCs and Apple computers and can hold 1,000 songs. It sold 125,000 units in its first three months, leading some commentators to herald it as the millennial equivalent of the Sony **WALKMAN**.

Some see the launch of this new generation of products as evidence of a new string being added to Apple's bow. Irene McWilliam, Professor of Computer Related Design at the Royal College of Art, argues that the new grail for IT manufacturers is 'connectivity'. According to McWilliam, electronic products need to be able to go 'through the loop of connectivity' – to successfully integrate with our software and all the other digital objects that have appeared in our lives – as well as to have their own integrity if they are to pass muster in our new techno-driven world.

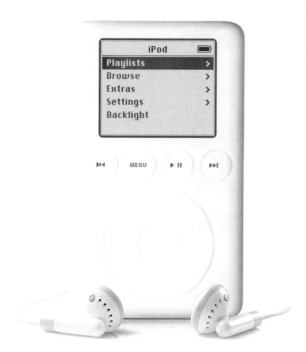

iPOD
Jonathan Ive and
Apple Design Team,
manufactured by Apple
Computing Inc., USA
2001–2

Other design insiders doubt whether Apple products do stand up to this sort of scrutiny. Tim Brown, CEO of the product-design company IDEO, argues that Apple's renaissance has been based on making computers beautiful rather than changing the way we think about them. 'Apple's achievement hasn't been about creating new kinds of behaviours,' says Brown. 'Theirs is the ultimate example of how to make technological objects desirable.'

Irene McWilliam, however, is convinced. 'Apple OS 10 [or OS X, the newest operating system] allows all the applications to work together; the interfaces synchronize and the objects look beautiful and work on their own or together,' she says. 'It's about people using the computer to orchestrate all the new digital objects that have appeared in their lives.' Experimental product designer Tony Dunne agrees, admitting that he has been seduced by a system that allows you to burn DVDs (with iDVD), edit, crop and organize your photos (with iPhoto) and turn all your CDs into MP3s (with iTunes). 'They've made the process of saving and using music effortless and enjoyable as well as making the laptop the hub around which everything else can revolve,' says Dunne. 'But it's not just an easy-to-use system; the objects themselves are beautiful.'

In a sense, the irony of all this is that while Apple's purple patch may have boosted its share price and its prestige – of all its launches since the iMac only the Cube has sunk without trace – its comeback has not increased the company's market share. It is true that people are buying more Apple computers than in the dark days of the early 1990s, but they are also buying more PCs. Apple's share of the world market is actually now down to 3 per cent from 5 per cent five years ago.

Apple has found its niche. If, however, it is to keep its title as the designer's innovator, the highly coordinated new-product-development process and the cross-functional collaborations with software, electrical engineering and mechanical design teams that underpinned the creation of the iPod will have to gather even more momentum. As Steve Jobs told 'Time' back in 2000, 'Victory in our industry is spelled survival. We're going to innovate our way out of this.' [16]

iMAC
Jonathan Ive and Apple Design Team,
manufactured by Apple Computing Inc.,
USA
2002

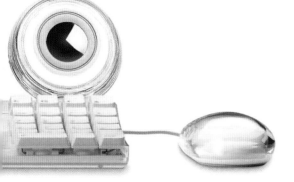

82–99

THE RISE AND FALL OF THE PDA

'IT'S LIKE BIODIVERSITY IN THE PRECAMBRIAN ERA, A WORLD TEEMING WITH RICH LIFE FORMS, MOST OF WHICH YOU KNOW VERY WELL WON'T SURVIVE.'

DENNIS BOYLE, IDEO

If ever a product epitomized the volatility of late-twentieth-century techno-entrepreneurism it is the Personal Digital Assistant (PDA), as a glance through Dennis Boyle's collection of 'electronic organizers' reveals. Boyle, a Senior Design Engineer in the Palo Alto, California office of product designers IDEO, has been passionate to the point of obsession about PDAs from the mid-1990s: 'It's been the most significant product of my professional life,' he says with feeling.

Boyle's passion has paid off. He has played a major part in the design evolution of two of the industry's most significant success stories, Palm and Handspring, helping to create an undisputed classic in the form of the **PALM V** in 2000. Yet as he enthusiastically digs through his bag of obsolete and obsolescent organizers, PDAs and pocket PCs, what is most striking is the narrow line between success and failure that most of these contenders have trodden. 'It's like biodiversity in the Precambrian era,' Boyle says as we examine products from Casio, Dell, Sony and Psion, assembled on IDEO's sunlit boardroom table. 'A world teeming with rich life forms, most of which you know very well won't survive…'

The Darwinian metaphor is an appropriate one. The PDA market was often a dynamic and profitable place in which to do business in the 1990s, but the hi-tech evolutionary landscape is also harsh and unforgiving. At least half of the products Boyle showed me failed to get going because they were overtaken by the competition, let down by functional shortcomings, or both. The ill-starred Apple Newton of 1993, for example, suffered from an unreliable operating system and was too big to fit in your pocket. In this volatile industry there is no room for resting on your laurels, either. In the early 1990s, for example, Psion controlled 90 per cent of the 'personal organizer' business. Now it no longer exists, at least as a hardware manufacturer.

THE YUPPIE FACTOR:
THE RISE OF PSION

There is a certain symmetry to this pattern of peaks and troughs. When Psion launched the **SERIES 3 ORGANIZER** in 1992, the product had in its turn supplanted a designer icon of its time. In the 1980s, 'personal organization' was done on paper and the field had one outstanding success story. With a system incorporating everything from spreadsheets to restaurant guides, the Filofax loose-leaf diary-cum-address book was the first organizer of the 'Lifestyle' era.

Psion's pocket-sized organizer did everything paper diaries did electronically and backed up the data safely in your PC. Moreover, these functional benefits came contained in a clamshell form that snapped neatly into action position, shutting with a businesslike little clunk. Here was an organizer for the 'paperless' executive, a desirable-looking machine that established itself instantly as a status symbol of the brave new digital world, eventually selling more than 1.5 million units in the mid-1990s.

Psion's breakthrough owed a good deal to product design. When the Series 3 was launched, the company had already been making its organizers for eight years. The company was the brainchild of British physicist David Potter, whose first commercial venture in computing was writing software for Sinclair computers. Its first portable computer was the 1984 Organizer, an electronic diary incorporating a basic database and one-line liquid-crystal display (LCD) screen for a proto-Yuppie it nicknamed 'Nigel'. According to the market profile, 'Nigel' would typically be 'aged 25–35, in middle to senior management, innovation-conscious, with lots of friends and contacts and a complicated life to organize'. [17]

ORGANIZER
Martin Riddiford/Frazer Designers, manufactured by Psion, UK
1984

PSION 3
Martin Riddiford/Frazer
Designers, manufactured
by Psion, UK
1991

Psion immediately had some success selling the product as a stock-checking tool to retail organizations such as Marks & Spencer, but the company's early efforts to make an electronic diary seemed less promising. Looking back, the plastic sleeve that contained the 1980s' machine, a sort of early take on the 'slider' mechanism now favoured by some mobile companies, seems clunky, and the alphabetical order of the keypad alien. It certainly didn't have the assurance to appeal to Yuppies accustomed to crocodile-leather-bound variants on the Filofax formula. Above all, though, it was the machine's scale – at fourteen by nine centimetres it was just that bit too big to warrant the 'pocket-sized' claim – which fatally undermined its 'aspirational' ambitions.

The Psion's gestation period as a consumer item was unusually long, but in other senses the pattern was one that became typical of the hi-tech field in the 1990s. 'Often the first iteration is about proving that a device works,' says Tim Brown, CEO of IDEO. 'The second is about making it desirable.'

The critical revision that led to the Psion becoming a desirable object came with the launch of the **PSION 3** in 1991, six years after the first machine had been made but still two years before Apple's then CEO John Sculley even coined the phrase 'Personal Digital Assistant'. (In preparing the ground for the forthcoming Apple Newton at a press conference in 1992, Sculley predicted that there was potentially a $3.5 million market for such computers.) The metamorphosis sprung from Psion's decision to split the unit into two parts, one side containing the screen and the other a standard 'qwerty' keyboard.

PSION 5
Martin
Riddiford/Therefore
Design, manufactured
by Psion, UK
1996

The designer chosen to undertake the redesign was Martin Riddiford, then of London consultacncy Frazer Designers, who had styled the previous version of the device. 'The only way to keep the Psion's form slim was to put the batteries in the spine,' Riddiford told me in 1998. 'So I came up with the idea of the double hinge. The idea is that when you open the machine the batteries flip out of the way, simultaneously making way for a support that tips the screen towards you.' But if the double-hinge mechanism was primarily about saving space, the cunning way it worked certainly added to the new Psion's appeal. 'It was intended to be as simple as possible because that's how I like design to be,' explains Riddiford. 'But I also wanted it to work in a way that intrigued you and drew you into using it.'

As miniaturization technology evolved over the next five years, Riddiford, now a partner with product designers and developers Therefore, continued to hone the Psion's form. By the time the **PSION 5** appeared in 1996, the machine had become a full-blown hand-held computer ten times more powerful than the Series 3. And it combined its 32-bit computer power with a brilliantly integrated sliding keyboard and an evolved clamshell hinge that made it stable for users to write on the touch-screen. But by then Psion's stranglehold on the market had long since been broken.

THE
EPIPHANY
OF PALM

Ironically, the product that was eventually to bounce Psion out of the PDA industry, the **PALM PILOT**, appeared to have considerably less design content than the slick-looking Psion when it first hit the shops in early 1996. Manufacturers Palm had retained industrial design consultancy Palo Alto Design Group to style the device in return for stock options, but even so the first product still had the air of a techie device. 'The Palm Pilot was battleship grey, the shell tended to crack and it looked very male. In fact, it projected geekiness,' says Dennis Boyle. 'I'd be walking around the office handing them out while David Kelley [IDEO's founder] would be calling out "Nerd! Nerd! Nerd!" to anyone who cared to listen.'

But while the Palm Pilot did not have the executive slickness of the Psion its inspired simplicity provided a critical edge. Palm's first PDA, the Zoomer, had been backed by Casio and Tandy until it was dropped in 1994, leaving Palm so strapped for cash that it had actually approached Psion with a proposal to develop 'connectivity software' that would allow Psion users to back up their machines on personal computers. The British company declined the offer, leaving Palm's founders Donna Dubinsky and Jeff Hawkins to look for other ways to develop their business plan.

It was clear that Jeff Hawkins had learned a great deal from the Zoomer. According to Rob Haitani, who designed the Palm Pilot interface, the Casio rejection was the catalyst for Hawkins' PDA 'epiphany'. 'The conventional wisdom was that you took a computer and shrunk it. But techy people tend to think too much about what technology can do rather than what you need it to do,' says Haitani. Hawkins' new starting point was that the PDA should be less a computer in its own right than an accessory to the PC which contained a basic diary, calendar and contact information. 'Jeff's concept was to jettison the unnecessary functions and put the 20 per cent of the features you needed in a little box that would fit in a shirt pocket and which was as fast and easy to use as a Filofax,' says Haitani. 'The idea was that it would synchronize with your computer, backing up all new information at the touch of a single button.'

When Palm's PDA reached the market two years later in February 1996, the results of this rationalization process were plain to see. The price – at $299 the Palm Pilot undercut anything else on the market – Haitani's interface (which always opened on the correct day and displayed a day's worth of appointments on a single screen) and the easy-to-use operating and touch-screen system were big pluses by comparison with the less than user-friendly Psion. The clincher, though, was the Hot Sync cradle that backed up your Palm Pilot every time you docked it. Suddenly a machine was available that removed at a stroke the one real reservation that all Psion owners had always had about their machines: the vulnerability of the information they contained.

The success of the Palm Pilot was therefore less about high design than it was about a brilliantly intuitive interface that made access to information quick, easy and reliable. By 1998, when Palm had sold 1.4 million of its Pilots and taken a grip on 70 per cent of the PDA market, the Silicon Valley pioneer seemed to have proved that, if the technology was clever enough you didn't need great product design to dominate the PDA market.

In the meantime, however, Jeff Hawkins had already decided that the looming spectre of a Microsoft PDA meant the time was ripe for a new sort of Palm. In 1997 Microsoft had launched its own PDA operating system so that Windows users could see a pared-down version of Windows 95 in what the company called Pocket PCs. Their strategy was to adopt Palm's simple form and interface but to trump the Californians by adding more computing power and a greater range of accessories.

AN ORGANIZING CLASSIC:
THE PALM V

In the same year, Palm had hired product designers IDEO to develop the form of a product code-named **RAZOR**. The idea was that, rather like Apple's iMac, the Razor would have very few extra technical features, relying instead for its impact on a slimline form and elegant presentation. 'Microsoft wanted a Pocket PC with more processing power than the Palm Pilot and there was a feeling in the market that they were capable of crushing us if we didn't act,' says Rob Haitani. 'The first generation of Palm was all about functionality. The second was all about design.' Jeff Hawkins agreed. 'I wanted to make it clear to everyone what the goal was,' Hawkins told Andrea Butter and David Pogue, co-authors of 'Piloting Palm', in 2002. 'The goal was beauty. Beauty, beauty, beauty. I didn't want any distraction with other things.'[18] The design upgrade proved particularly timely bearing in mind the growing design-driven competition that Palm was soon to face from other PDAs.

By the beginning of the millennium, Microsoft's strategy was beginning to have an impact – thanks in part to investment in product design. The Microsoft-powered manufacturer Compaq had commissioned product-design consultancy Astro Design to create an eye-catching design for its own new pocket PC, the **iPAQ**. 'The brief from Compaq was to design a Palm Killer,' says Kyle Swen, Manager of Astro Design's San Francisco studio. Svelte in form and silver in colour, with sleeves that snapped on to hold different kinds of accessories, the iPaq also featured the first full-colour screen. It quickly became a cult object, if not a big seller, on its own account after its launch in July 2000.

PAGER/PDA (prototype)
Samsung Design Europe,
Samsung, UK
2001

Fortunately for Palm the design overhaul that it had undergone at IDEO's hands protected it from Swen's 'Palm Killer'. Dennis Boyle had revised the design by addressing the main flaws of the Palm Pilot one by one and making a series of prototypes that he passed out to friends to test and report back on. Its slim, heat-blasted aluminium body – more robust than that of its ancestor – added a new strand of desirability to the **PALM V** (see p.38), which was soon paying back the investment in design. Meanwhile, a new series of mix-and-match accessories, such as an alligator-skin cover, provided extra feminine appeal. Despite a price tag that was $50 more than that of any other of the company's products, the Palm V was soon winning rave reviews and new customers. Within a year of its launch in February 2000, the Palm V accounted for half the products the company sold.

The rebirth of the Palm in its new designer clothing was a triumph both for the manufacturers and for Dennis Boyle and his team, but by the end of 2000, Palm was facing its first real competition. Alongside the Microsoft Pocket PCs, Sony had launched its own Palm OS-powered machine, the Clié, and the company was even facing competition of its own making. The launch of the Palm Pilot had been funded by US Robotics, but in 1997 that company had merged with the $3-billion networking giant 3 Com. By 1999, Palm founders Jeff Hawkins and Donna Dubinsky had had enough of the corporate politics that ensued. In June 1999, they left Palm along with twelve of the original senior management team to found their own PDA manufacturer, Handspring. By the end of 2000, Handspring already had four of its own PDAs on the market.

PDA EXPANSIONISM: HANDSPRING AND THE VISOR

At first the launch of Hawkins' new model company – and its first product, the **HANDSPRING VISOR** – appeared to herald the start of a new era for the PDA that combined distinctive innovation with high-quality design. Jeff Hawkins had observed the booming state of the mobile phone market. He was convinced that the future for the PDA lay in combining its existing strengths – the calendar, contact and notepad functions – with the facility to communicate not just on the Internet but also by voice. The problem was that moving into the communicator business was far too big a project for a start-up company short of cash to take on.

Instead, Handspring came up with what initially looked like a brilliant compromise: their first product, the Visor, featured an 'expansion slot' that accepted a variety of plug-in modules that enabled the PDA to interface with a string of accessories such as wireless modems, pagers, MP3 players and games. The principle was that the Springboard expansion slot provided opportunities for companies to partner with Handspring and add modular applications, thus buying Handspring the time to develop the 'Visorphone' of Hawkins' dreams.

The strategy looked like a winner. IDEO's industrial designers and electrical and mechanical engineers had spent a year honing both the form and the mechanical design of the Visor. IDEO had even taken a punt on a Handspring accessory of its own, a camera. When it was launched, the playful looking blue polycarbonate body and the low price seemed set to do for PDAs what the iMac was doing for PCs. Soon, Handspring had snapped up a quarter of the US PDA market.

HANDSPRING VISOR
IDEO
manufactured by
Handspring, USA
2000

FROM SPRING TO SLUMP: PDAS IN DECLINE

As things turned out, the year 2000 turned out to be less the start of something big than the high-water mark for PDAs. With the sudden bursting of the dot-com bubble that came in that millennial summer, sales of PDAs began to drift into decline. Handspring's Visorphone, launched in the autumn of 2000, quickly flopped, and the trickle of plug-in modules that the company had expected to become a flood dried up.

Meanwhile the **VISOR EDGE**, Handspring's sleek upmarket model, also foundered when it was launched in March 2001, undercut by stocks of its Palm counterpart the **PALM VX**, a machine which, thanks to discounting, now cost $100 less. 'We had great hopes for the Handspring but as it turned out, the expandable concept didn't have enough life force,' admits Dennis Boyle. 'Since then everyone has been trying to figure out what the sweet spot is in a maturing PDA market.'

That is not to say that PDAs have entirely lost their charm for the public. Their ever-improving functionality has won them new supporters in certain sectors. As predicted by Philips' Dr Shiva concept from Visions of the Future in 1995, they have a substantial fan club among medical practitioners, for example. Mohammed Al-Ubaydli is a specialist in digital information in the field. 'PDAs are important because of the way clinicians spend most of their day – walking, from patient to patient, ward to ward and department to department,' he says. 'They are extremely light, fit into a clinician's pocket, have long battery life, switch on immediately and do not crash. All of these properties are extremely important for the busy mobile work style of clinicians.'

VISOR EDGE
IDEO
manufactured by Handspring,
USA
2001

Substantial though it may be, however, this niche application is no more likely to save the PDA as a mass-market consumer device than Apple's school computer, the eMate, was likely to save that company in the mid-1990s. At the time of writing, there are something like 120 PDAs on the market. Sony alone has launched over a dozen new versions of its Clié in the past year and Hewlett Packard has emerged as the dynamic force in the business market. If pioneers such as Palm and Handspring are to successfully battle with giant competitors such as Microsoft and to survive in a marketplace that looks increasingly crowded, they need their equivalent of the iMac. The difficulty, of course, is that since every manufacturer has now invested in it, product design is no longer enough to allow a PDA to stand out.

Irene McWilliam, Professor of Computer Related Design at the Royal College of Art, is one commentator who believes that the PDA is on the verge of obsolescence. She argues that the device is now caught in a deadly pincer movement between ever-more compact personal computers and ever-more versatile mobile phones. Technology commentator Dave Birch agrees, pointing out that the world market for PDAs continues to spiral downwards, falling by a quarter in 2002: 'It could be that their [PDAs'] space is disappearing. People don't need them anymore…' Birch wrote in the 'Guardian' in May 2003. 'Once I could synchronize my phone with my laptop, I started to forget the PDA.' [19]

HIPTOP
Thomas Meyerhoffer
manufactured by Danger, USA
2002

ADAPT OR DIE: FROM PALM TO HIPTOP

If the pioneers of Silicon Valley are to stage a fightback they will have to rethink their innovation strategies. In this sense, the **HIPTOP**, a new device from Danger, another Palo-Alto-based Silicon Valley start-up, may provide one beacon of hope. The Hiptop is still a PDA, but one that is based less on the principles of computing than on those of telecommunications. As Handspring and Palm struggle to persuade customers to shell out between $300 and $500 on their products, Danger customers can buy the Hiptop, a device that allows them to surf the Internet, send emails, take, send and receive pictures, play games and make phone calls for just $50.

The secret is that, unlike other PDAs, the Hiptop contains no hard disk. Instead, those who buy it also sign up to a dedicated Hiptop server for which they pay a monthly fee that is shared by one of the major telecom network providers and by Hiptop itself. 'What everyone else has out there is a scaled down PC,' explains Danger's Design Director Matias Duarte. 'Our philosophy looks at the thing from the other end of the telescope. The philosophy is about making the server do all the work. Our business is about making the product attractive enough that you want to subscribe.'

The Hiptop is also pitched at a rather different sort of audience from the executives who have usually represented the heart of the PDA market, a strategy that is reflected in its visual character and shape created by Thomas Meyerhoffer, who designed the Newton when he was at Apple. 'The Hiptop is pitched at the leisure and communication interests of 16–34 year olds,' says Duarte. 'So it has an emotional character and functional form which is appropriate to them.'

With its curvy retro-modern form and its screen that spins out to reveal a mini keyboard beneath clearly conceived for veteran thumbers, the Hiptop looks a bit like a Psion for the youth market. 'A lot of PDA design seems a bit frigid,' says Duarte. 'I wanted to evoke a vision of the future to create the sort of futuristic but appealing object that you might have seen in '2001, A Space Odyssey.'

'DFB' PERSONAL DIGITAL ASSISTANT
(prototype)
Pentagram, for Hewlett Packard, USA
2002

PHONEBOOK
Therefore Design, manufactured
by Inventec, China
2003

It remains to be seen, of course, if Danger can pick up the subscribers who will make its dream of a new model PDA work. Twelve months after the launch of the Hiptop, Danger has picked up the 'Wired' prize for innovation and is still in business, but even at this stage the company is still declining to reveal its subscriber numbers. Dennis Boyle of IDEO still believes that that the PDA has a vital role to play as the all-round communicator of the future. 'In ten years we will have these amazing tools right on our bodies. They will be on our belts, our watches, our glasses and in our pockets,' he says. 'They'll have voice and text capabilities and let us surf the Net at high speed.'

Boyle may be right, and the Hiptop shows that California's spirit of enterprise and daring is still alive and kicking. Yet Palm's decision to buy back Handspring in the summer of 2003 reveals the difficulties that West Coast innovators now face in a global marketplace. Always niche products more popular with men than women, PDAs are now competing on the territory occupied by mobile phones. Even if the reunified Palm has the technological know-how, it is hard to believe that it has the global branding, marketing and distribution resources to persuade the public to opt for a Palm product rather than one made by big mobile phone brands like Nokia, Motorola or Samsung. Products like Handspring's Treo 'communicator' – featuring an awkward qwerty keyboard for use with one finger – really don't look the part at all.

Although Silicon Valley may now have played its part as the key mover and shaker in the evolution of the PDA, those in the know believe that it won't be long before the inventors are making a comeback. 'Whatever becomes of the PDA, you can be sure that five years down the line Jeff Hawkins will be floating some other brilliant new technological concept in the marketplace', says Tim Brown, CEO of IDEO. 'That's the nature of Silicon Valley innovators. They just keep on bouncing back.'

REINVENTING THE PHONE: FROM TALKING BRICKS TO FASHION-TECH

'AS A PRODUCT DESIGNER IT'S UNUSUAL TO GET THE CHANCE TO DEFINE THE CHARACTER OF AN ENTIRELY NEW PRODUCT.'

FRANK NUOVO, NOKIA

MOTOROLA 'BRICK'
DynaTAC phone (prototype)
1973
© 2003 Motorola Archives

MOTOROLA HANDIE-TALKIE ADVERT
1944
© 2003 Motorola Archives

When Frank Nuovo set about creating his first mobile phone back in the late 1980s, he started with the proverbial blank page. 'As a product designer it's unusual to get the chance to define the character of an entirely new product,' Nuovo recalled when I met him in 2003. In a sense the mobile phone was not 'entirely new'. Motorola's two-way AM radio, the **HANDIE-TALKIE**, and the FM backpack version, the Walkie-Talkie, were potent symbols of American military technology during the Second World War. Over the next half century, the American company remained one of the pioneers in paging and mobile phone technology, creating the first brick-like portable cellular handset in 1984. But Nuovo's primary source of ideas for the mobile as a consumer object was less the past than a sci-fi vision of the future. 'My inspirations were the 'Star Trek' gizmos that I had loved as a child: the Tri-Corder and the Communicator,' he said.

A designer with a brief to design a mobile would hardly be short of design sources today. Nuovo is now the Design Director of Nokia, the world's leading global manufacturer, with around 40 per cent of the mobile phone market. He now oversees a pan-global new-product-development group and has separate creative teams at his disposal in Beijing, Tokyo, London, Dallas and Helsinki. The designers on these teams spend much of their time dreaming up future consumer scenarios for mobile technology products and accessories of all kinds.

MOTOROLA V50
manufactured by Motorola,
Scotland and Germany,
2001

This is all part of a segmented approach to the design and marketing of mobile phones that cater for their users' specific interests and moods as well as for the functional requirements of business, work or pleasure contexts. Nokia ranges now encompass from Premium at the top, through Fashion, Classic, Expression, Active and Basic. In each case the typical customer's taste and behaviour is defined in some detail. Nokia's 'Fashion' customers, for example, are divided into 'experiencers' and 'impressors... urban trendsetters with high shopping spending. Unisex with female bias. Early stages of professional life. Merge work and play with an active night life. Prioritize uniqueness and creativity.'[20]

This may just be the start. Nuovo believes that the future of the mobile phone lies in more specialization. He predicts the emergence of more phones-cum-organizers for business people, 'boutique' phones for fashion victims, 'console' phones for gamers and so on. 'There will be much more focus on devices with specific and unique functions,' Nuovo predicts, illustrating the point with a good old down-home metaphor. 'You don't use your sedan to collect lumber.'

Nokia's approach to mobile phone design and marketing has gained currency in the past five years. Siemens Mobile, which now vies with Samsung for the position of the world's fourth biggest mobile phone maker, has also divided its products into four groups. These borrow their titles from Mercedes and their character is intended to appeal to the customer targeted by each of the German automobile manufacturer car 'classes'. From the bottom up, 'A' is Siemens' basic range; 'C' a section that is focused on fashionable products on a budget; 'M' the sporty range and 'S' the pricey, premium collection. Siemens Mobile's Design Director Uli Skrypalle is unapologetic about the debt his design approach owes to Nokia. 'They're the market leader so it can't be too far wrong, can it?' he says.

MY PHONE IS WHO I AM: MOBILES AS CULTURAL ACCESSORIES

If mobile phones do indeed acquire highly specialized functions over the next few years, it is improbable that they will do so at the expense of styling or image. It doesn't seem to matter whether the context is London or Lagos; for young, design-conscious mobile phone owners in the First or Third Worlds, every detail of their phone is an issue central to their personal identity: the colour and shape of the handset, the ring tone and even, in the case of Japanese buyers, the strap to which it is attached. Motorola went as far as to commission a lengthy anthropological study devoted to assessing the mobile phone impact on social and individual life, which invited readers to categorize their mobile habits as those of a 'flashy peacock', a 'chattering sparrow' or a 'solitary owl'.[21]

In a special report in 2002 dedicated to celebrating the mobile phone's significance, 'Guardian' fashion writer Jess Cartner-Morley characterized the mobile as the 'key cultural accessory' of the era, an object that epitomized the era as the trainer did the mid-1990s.[22] It was, she argued, 'a product that tallies precisely with the cultural aspirations of the moment… the means by which owner pronounced him or herself to be au fait with the modern world'.

The mobile phone's new-found status as a 'key cultural accessory' explains why fashion styling has been such an important issue for product designers during the mobile's fifteen-year metamorphosis from primitive communicator to trend-sensitive mass-made object. Even Siemens, hardly the most glamour-conscious of international electronics companies, is now presenting itself as a fashion brand. At the New York launch of its **S55** mobile phone in October 2002, the company's Design Director Uli Skrypalle revealed that the washboard-style number keypad had an unusual source of inspiration. 'I told them it was inspired by the six-pack tummy muscles of Marky Mark the model and (as Mark Wahlberg) Hollywood actor,' says Skrypalle. 'Now it's the thing that everyone seems to remember about the phone.'

SIEMENS S55
manufactured by Siemens, Germany,
2002

SIEMENS SL55
manufactured by Siemens, Germany,
2003

With its cute 'slider' format, trendy colours ('ruby' or 'titanium'), 'polyphonic' sixteen-chord ring tone and 'jewel-like' concealed keypad, the S55's dinky companion phone, the **SL55**, is pushing its credentials as a digital fashion statement even harder. Siemens even issued a special press release reporting which B and C list Hollywood stars – from Kevin Costner to Andie MacDowell – had been spotted at the Cannes Film Festival using an SL55. 'We have to target the fashion-conscious people,' says Uli Skrypalle.

DEFYING THE TECHNOLOGY STEROTYPE: THE RISE OF NOKIA

In 2002 Nokia made 5.4 billion Euros on sales of 30 billion Euros and the company anticipates there will be 1.6 billion mobile phone users at the end of 2005 as against 1.2 billion in 2003.[23] Given both the potential for huge profits and the predicted expansion of the market, it's hardly surprising that manufacturers are throwing money at design. Yet in a sense the identity of the world's leading mobile phone manufacturer is surprising. Nokia hardly fits the technology stereotype, being from neither Silicon Valley nor the Far East. Rather, this little-known company from (as the Finns themselves say) 'behind God's back' was an industrial conglomerate making paper, rubber, cables and then electronics for most of the twentieth century, emerging as a player in the nascent mobile industry in the late 1980s.

Since then, the company has established itself as the dominant force in the second-generation cellular industry. In 1998 it overtook Motorola, the company that claims it invented mobile technology fifty years ago. By 2002, Nokia claimed its share of the world mobile phone market had grown to 38 per cent – around 15 per cent more than that of its nearest rival.

Most of the credit for Nokia's innovation philosophy and the global research and development and product-development policies that have underpinned its success belongs to the single-mindedness and meticulous planning of its Finnish senior management, in particular to its ambitious CEO Jorma Ollila. But design has been a significant factor. In his book 'The Nokia Revolution', Dan Steinbock suggests that the Finnishness of its product style has contributed significantly to the extraordinary rise of the company. 'Just as Marimekko had rethought the idea of the dress, Nokia rethought the idea of the telephone.'[24]

Perhaps the Finns had an intuitive grasp of the edge that design might give them in gaining consumer acceptance and popularity. It would, however, be hard to argue that either the objects or the interface owe much to Scandinavia. Frank Nuovo is the Design Director usually credited with creating the visual character of Nokia's ranges and a man who 'Vogue' has described as 'the man who made wireless technology a fashion statement'. Nuovo flies to Finland almost every month, but he has never lived in Finland and would appear to owe more influence to 'Star Trek's' Gene Roddenberry than to Finland's roll call of twentieth-century Modernists like Kaj Franck, Tapio Wirkkala or Alvar Aalto.

Nuovo, a one-time jazz musician from the arty town of Monterey, comes across as the quintessential Californian creative, arguing that the West Coast is the perfect place for a phone designer to grow up in and to find inspiration. 'In California you can be skiing in the morning and surfing in the afternoon,' he says. 'The culture is all about entertainment and mobility.'

NOKIA 101
Designed and manufactured
by Nokia, Finland
1992

FROM
BLACK BRICKS
TO STAR TREK:
1990S'
MOBILE DESIGN
CULTURE

Nuovo began working with Nokia as a consultant for the LA-based design agency DesignWorks in 1989. He admits that he had a mission to stamp his personality on the mobile from the start. In the early years, however, there was precious little evidence of a spirit of adventure in the form of the company's products. Nokia's early efforts, such as the **NOKIA 101** or **121**, shared the rectilinear and brick-like character that was common to all the phones of the era. As late as 1993, long after the mobile became 'jacket-pocketable', even a Siemens' 'blue sky' styling exercise produced concepts that, but for the odd expressive curve, were no more than functional boxes.

It is understandable that mobile designers took a while to develop a feel for the phone. When the first commercial mobile phones were appearing in the late 1980s, techno-culture – and techno-capitalism – as we have come to understand it today was still more a dream than a reality. True, the PC had established itself as a staple feature of the working environment, but the laptop was still a novelty and the PDA nothing more than a gleam in its creator's eye.

The mobile phone also made an unlikely sort of design pioneer considering the conservatism that had characterized the evolution of its traditional land-lined cousin. Telephones were rarely characterized by adventurous styling until the deregulation of telecommunication markets. There were odd exceptions, such as the 1960s' British-designed Trimphone, but due largely to restrictions on the licensing of phone technology, even late in the twentieth century manufacturing design was still struggling to shake off the weight of history. Henry Dreyfuss' classic handset design for Bell created in 1937 was still the industry standard telephone in the late 1980s.

At last, with the Nokia 2110 of 1994, Nuovo was permitted to take a few liberties with the boxy shape of the phone. He responded by increasing the size of the unit to accommodate an elliptical 'bubble' surrounded by a TV-style bezel that framed the screen, the control button and the send and receive keys. The combination of curves and natural intelligibility made the **NOKIA 2110** an immediate hit. 'It was meant to be a friendly companion rather than just a square box,' says Nuovo.

The success of the 2110 won Nuovo his position as Nokia's in-house Design Director in 1995 and established the basic 'candy bar' (as distinct from the 'slider' or 'flip-top') format and the key layout that Nokia has favoured ever since. Even after Nuovo's entry into the Nokia hierarchy, however, his lifestyle vision of the phone was still considered dangerously radical by the top management. 'When I said I wanted to make phones that were fun and that reflected people's personalities in the way that fashion accessories do, people looked at me as if I shouldn't be saying that kind of thing,' he recalls. 'Back then it was still all about the technology.'

NOKIA 2110
Designed and manufactured
by Nokia, Finland
1994

REFLECTING YOUR MOBILE MOOD: GRAPHICS BECOME THE LOOK

When, seven years after his first Nokia concept, Nuovo did finally get his chance to create a fashion-focused mobile phone, his lifestyle take on the object immediately paid off. At a distance of eight years the concept behind the **NOKIA 5110** and the **3210** seems extraordinarily simple. Both models retained most of the established format that Nokia had already established. The key difference was decorative. The Nokia 5110 featured a front-face removable graphic cover with designs like the Stars and Stripes, which you could 'change to reflect your mood'. The 3210 that followed had images on the front and the back. 'The graphics became the look,' says Nuovo simply.

All phones on this spread designed and manufactured by Nokia, Finland

NOKIA 5110
1998

Simple they may have been, but the immediate popularity of removable covers sparked such a sales surge that Nokia was able to steal a march on competitors such as Ericsson and Motorola, who were still preoccupied with their phones' technical specifications. His credibility bolstered by this success, Nuovo played the fashion card. The launch of the premium-priced **NOKIA 8210**, a dinky chrome-coloured model consciously intended to resemble a piece of jewellery, further boosted his profile.

For the launch, Nuovo shrewdly commissioned a special suit by fashion designer Jhane Barnes featuring a special integral pocket for the phone; he immediately found himself feted as a celebrity. Soon even the fashion press was waxing lyrical. The **NOKIA 8850** was, American 'Vogue' gushed, 'a little Le Corbusier, a little Matrix…it looks as if it were made to be retrieved chirping from a clutch purse…the perfect neo-80s status thing.'[25] 'I did the talk-show circuit for that one,' he recalls. 'That was when I coined the phrase fashion-tech for a product that applies fashion values to technology culture.'

NOKIA 3210
1999

NOKIA 8210
2000

NOKIA 8850
1999

FORM FOLLOWS FUN:
THE CONVERSION OF SIEMENS

For all Nokia's success it seems surprising that so few of the company's rivals appear to have responded to the new product imperative as efficiently as the Finns. Perhaps the difficulty experienced by the competition in coming to terms with the new consumerist realities had something to do with their engineering-focused backgrounds.

Uli Skrypalle, Design Director at Siemens Mobile, admits that for much of the 1990s the German giant was held back by the unfamiliarity of the territory. 'Siemens is a very technically oriented company which has tended to follow the traditional Modernist design dictum that form follows function. But that isn't the way the world works anymore,' Skrypalle admits. 'We live in a pluralistic era in which no firm rules about styling apply. That's why we had to restructure our thinking about mobile design so that we could create designs which follow fun, emotion and lifestyle and which draw on the many visual references that people have in their lives.'

For the past five years, Skrypalle has been trying to make up for lost time, building an independently operating design team based in its own large studio in Munich, which serves as a think tank for the company's mobile products. An open admirer of Nokia, Skrypalle tacitly acknowledges the influence he owes to the Finnish company. Like Nuovo, Skrypalle oversees culturally diverse design teams in the US (Seattle and Silicon Valley), Europe (both in Germany) and China. Like Nuovo, he views greater specialization as the way forwards.

Nokia's 'N-Gage' introduced in February 2003, and similar entertainment-focused products by Sony Ericsson and Samsung, illustrate the thinking. It is possible to make a phone call by flipping the N-Gage onto its side, but with its fan-shaped form, big colour screen and symmetrical 'left-right' ten-digit keypad – clearly created for veteran 'thumbers' and resembling a Nintendo games console – the N-Gage's primary function is as a gaming device. 'Stylistically and functionally it's a machine based on gaming,' says Nuovo. 'It puts all the gaming manufacturers on notice that we're in the heart of their territory.'

N-GAGE
specialist fan-shaped gaming phone with
large colour screen and symmetrical 'left-
right' ten-digit keypad
manufactured by Nokia, Finland
2003

VERTU HANDSET
Frank Nuovo, manufactured by Vertu, UK
2002

THE MOBILE
STATUS SYMBOL:

VERTU,
XELEBRI AND
MINIMALISM

It all sounds logical enough, but Nokia's launch of Vertu at the beginning of 2002 is a different matter. Frank Nuovo is himself Creative Director of the independent Nokia subsidiary based in the Hampshire (UK) town of Church Crookham, which is dedicated to making luxury mobile phones. But the high-profile advertising campaign for the new product lacks real conviction. Can there really, one wonders, be much of a market for an Art Deco-influenced mobile phone priced at an astonishing £14,950 and featuring a sapphire face and a body available in platinum, white gold or stainless steel?

Nuovo believes that there is a market for a mobile with Cartier overtones. 'When I go swimming in Hawaii I wear a different watch to the one I have when I'm working in the yard so why shouldn't the same apply to mobiles?' he reasons. 'Vertu is about craftsmanship and I wanted to be able to pioneer my craft. It's a piece of art in the same way that a beautiful watch is. And the technology is designed to be upgradeable.'

Vertu represented an attempt on the part of the brand of choice to claim the high ground of design as its own. But a year or two on, the ploy was looking as if it had backfired. It is undeniable that the trend-forecasting, user-friendly interface and slick styling that Nuovo had championed were proving a potent mass-market combination, but you cannot help wondering if Nokia's Design Director had begun to believe his own publicity.

Nokia's success has been solidly based on shrewd marketing and highly efficient and truly globalized development, production and distribution policies. As for design, Nokia's simple and intelligible interface remains the best on the market, but the company cannot really claim to have produced an undisputed product classic in the five years since its domination of the industry began.

Even the amiable Uli Skrypalle has his doubts about the notion of applying the rules of the collectors' item to an object that is sometimes seen as almost disposable. 'I don't believe it's possible to think that you can make an object like a mobile phone upgradeable to the needs of new technology,' says Skrypalle. 'Too many things can change.' Siemens' response to the mobile-fashion addict targeted by Vertu was a range of three mobiles called **XELEBRI**. Like Vertu, these were intended to be sold as clothing accessories. In fashion shops the whimsy comes at a much more affordable price than Vertu's cheapest option, the stainless steel model at around £5,000.

You might even argue that the Finnish company never looked quite as vulnerable to its product-design opposition as it did in the summer of 2003. As its stylized range was compared unfavourably to a modish and minimal series of product introductions from its rivals, there was even talk of 'Nokia fatigue'.

There are persistent rumours that Nokia's next generation of handsets will be more in line with the understated look that has become the mobile design orthodoxy.

LUNAR XELEBRI
manufactured by Siemens, Germany
2002

V70 MOBILE PHONE
manufactured by Motorola, USA
2002

TALBY PHONE
Marc Newson, manufactured by KDDI, Japan
2003

Motorola, historically the technological innovator, appears to have co-opted minimal design into its campaign to claw back the ground it lost to Nokia in the 1990s. Tim Parsey, Motorola's Chicago-based Design Director, admits that Apple 'fits into every conversation about design trends we're having'. Parsey's preoccupation in 2003 was with the 'power of simplicity'. 'There's a move away from the surface into things that have substance to them. It is a move to enjoying the power of simplicity made possible because there is phenomenal inventiveness in materials,' says Parsey. 'We've gone through the era of, "Hey that looks modern!", both in terms of the interface and the physical aspect. Now it's about using time to think how to do other things. There is a need to think about purity of product expression in order to allow you to go crazy in the other areas.'

Other new designs reinforced this sense of Nokia as the odd manufacturer out. Samsung continued to gain market share thanks to the popularity of its elegant **V200** flip-top. Sony Ericsson appeared to have mounted the minimal bandwagon too. Since Ericsson joined forces with Sony in October 2001 to become Sony Ericsson, the company has rethought its design policy from scratch. Japanese Design Director Hiroshi Nakaizumi has drawn up a new policy for the company based on 'human centred design', 'appeal to the sixth sense' and 'being half a step ahead of the consumer'. [26] The results, including the **T610** and several flip-top designs, have caught the eye.

SONY ERICSSON T610
manufactured by
Sony Erricson,
2003

V200 MOBILE PHONE
Designed by Samsung Design
Office, Seoul
2000

NEW MOBILE
CHALLENGES:
RETHINKING
THE THIRD
GENERATION

You sense that – in terms of marketing if not market share – the gap between Nokia and companies that aspire to its success has begun to close. Perhaps the key to the progress of these companies has been their receptiveness to new ideas. Siemens is a case in point. The company's initiatives include an in-house design lab, an annual scholarship scheme that invites ten top design students from around the world to Munich to spend a year dreaming up wild and wonderful notions for the mobile's future. Should it incorporate a video recorder, a Global Positioning System (GPS), an MP3 player or all three, for example?

Uli Skrypalle has also built a strong network of outside consultants – from product designers to fashion specialists – whom he regularly calls on for ideas, and he continues to be open to strategic alliances wherever he finds them. 'I think we have to find appropriate partners that complement our strengths and fit the functionality of the product,' says Skrypalle. 'That might mean linking up with Prada to do a fashion product or with Adidas to do an active phone. The one thing that we can't afford to do is nothing.'

Skrypalle is right there. In a sense, it hasn't been entirely surprising that mobile phone manufacturers made such a feature of fashion in the early years of the twenty-first century. It's true that texting became a phenomenon in the early 'noughties' (between 2002 and 2003 the number of text messages sent globally was expected to grow from 300 to 450 billion), and that mobiles integrating cameras and gaming devices also became common. But the real leaps in mobile phone technology will happen if and when all-singing, all-dancing universal standard third generation (3G) mobile technology finally arrives.

LEATHER CASED PHONE
(design concept)
Siemens Design Lab, for Siemens, Germany
2002
→

3G ELECTRONIC FILOFAX (PROTOTYPE)
Samsung Design Europe,
for Samsung, UK
2000

There has been a series of false starts for 3G in the past few years. Now, however, almost every manufacturer has a 3G handset on the market and we may just be on the brink of the much-anticipated boom. If and when the boom does come it may bring tumultuous change in its wake. According to a report by the British research organization Demos, 3G will give mobile phones capabilities that will knock those of our second-generation devices into a cocked hat. Successful mobile phone manufacturers with the right specialized products will be able extend their business further into imaging, music and other services that require streaming sound and video.[27]

More importantly, Demos argues, if consumers are prepared to embrace them fully, 3G mobiles could far transcend their commercial and communication functions. The London-based think tank argues that 3G mobiles could even help governments to deliver public services such as transport, education and health more efficiently. As one example, Demos cites a collaboration between network provider O2 and Oxford University that uses a 3G phone to monitor an asthma patient's health. 'As a new generation of mobile technologies takes off,' the Demos report argues, 'the social potential of the mobile will vastly increase.'

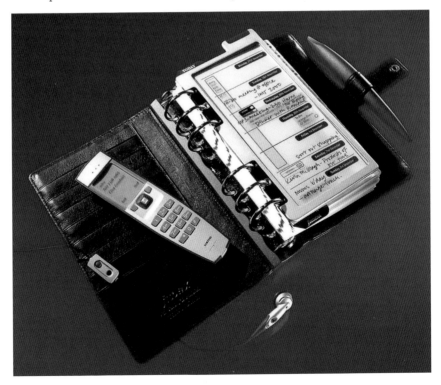

3G COMPACT PHONE
(prototype)
Samsung Design Europe,
for Samsung, UK
2000

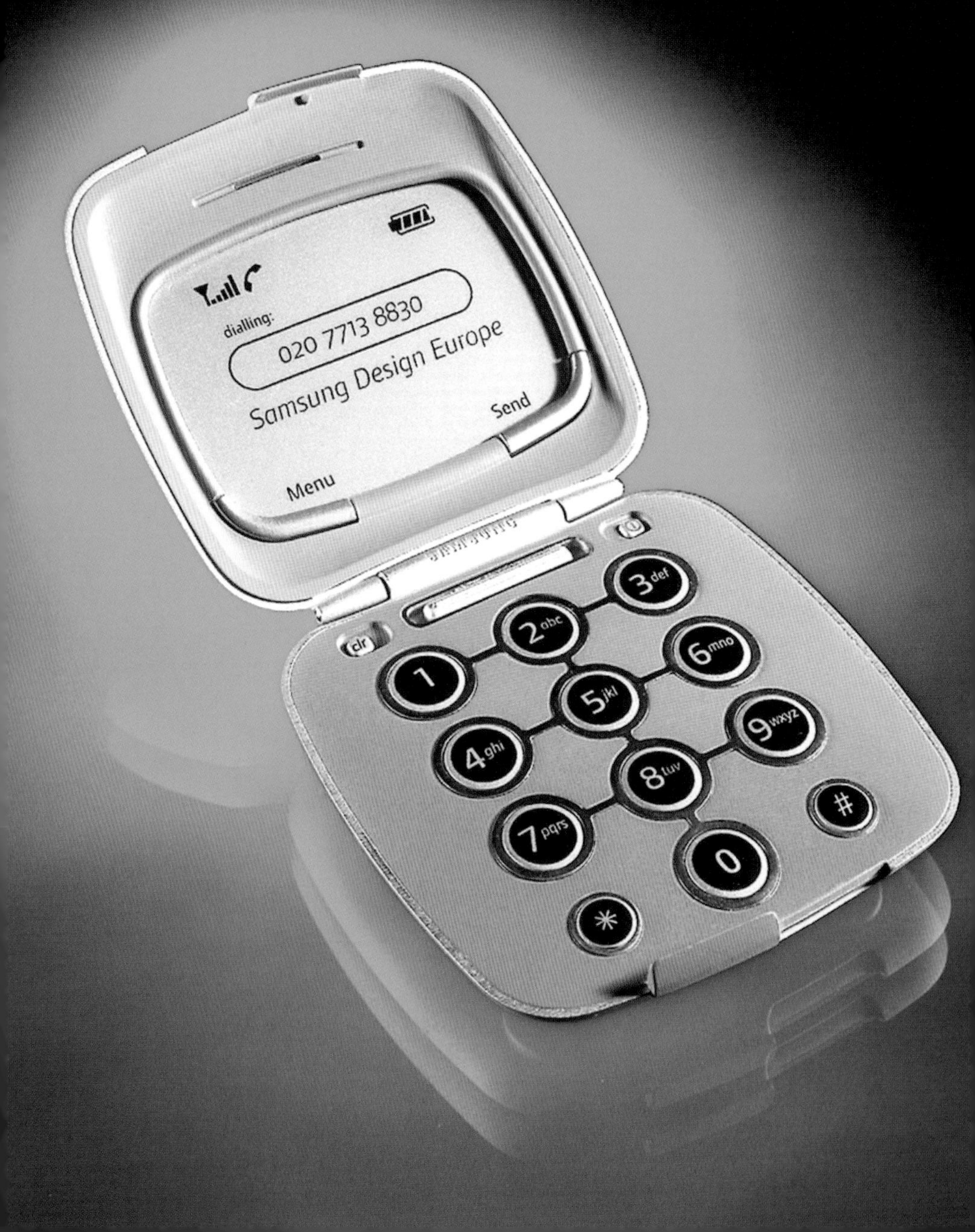

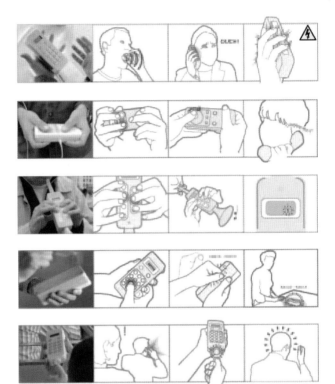

Not before time, you might think. Despite its ubiquity and convenience, we haven't yet learned to love the mobile phone. Its disruptiveness even led IDEO to propose a collection of Social Mobiles that respond to the frustration and anger caused by other people's phones. The **SOMO1** discourages inappropriate noisiness by administering an electric shock to its users if they speak too loudly. Like me, you have probably wished a SoMo1 shock on someone somewhere at some time. Indispensable companions they may be, but mobile phones continue to be one of the least popular inventions of modern times – at least when they're in the hands of other people.

So far the shiny and superficial machines that the forces of fashion and marketing have created have done little to shift this antisocial image. If manufacturers and their product and interface designers are to turn the mobile phone into the subtle 'unreservedly positive' force Demos anticipate, they will have to think a good deal deeper about 3G technology than they seemed to about the first and second generations. We can only hope that they are capable of rising to the challenge.

124
FURTHER RESEARCH

Butter, Andrea and Pogue, David, Piloting Palm: the Inside Story of Palm, Handspring and the Birth of the Billion Dollar Handheld Industry, John Wiley & Sons, New York, 2002

Cairncross, Frances, The Death of Distance: how the communication revolution will change our lives, Orion Business Books, London, 1997

Carlton, Jim, Apple: the Inside Story of Intrigue, Egomania and Business Blunders, Century Business Books, USA, 1997

Davey, Andrew, Detail: exceptional Japanese product design, Laurence King, London, 2003

Dunne, Anthony, Hertzian Tales: electronic products, aesthetic experience and critical design, RCA Computer Related Design Research, London, 1999

Dunne, Anthony and Raby, Fiona, Design Noir: the secret life of electronic objects, August/Birkhauser, Switzerland, 2002

Fiell, Charlotte and Peter, Designing the 21st century, Taschen, London, 2002

Gershenfeld, Neil, When Things Start to Think, Coronet, London, 1999

Grinyer, Clive, Smart Design: products that change our lives, Rotovision, Switzerland, 2001

Julier, Guy, The Culture of Design, Sage Publications, London, 2000

Moore, Geoffrey, Crossing the Chasm: marketing and selling technology products to mainstream customers, Capstone Publishing, New York, 1999

Myerson, Jeremy (ed.), Rewind: 40 Years of D&AD, Phaidon, London, 2002

Norman, Donald A., Emotional Design: why we love (or hate) everyday things, Basic Books, New York, 2004

Pavitt, Jane (ed.), Brand.New, V&A Publications, London, 2000

Pedersen, Martin, Apple Design: the work of the Apple Industrial Design Group, Graphis, New York, 1997

Philips, Visions of the Future, exhibition catalogue, V&K Publishing, Blaricum, The Netherlands, 1996

Redhead, David, Products of our Time, August/Birkhauser, Switzerland, 1999

Redhead, David, The Power of 10: ten products by ten British product designers, Laurence King, London, 2001

Steinbock, Dan, The Nokia Revolution, Amacom, New York, 2001

Thackara, John & Jane, Stuart, New British Design, Thames & Hudson, London, 1987

Thackara, John (ed.), Design after Modernism: beyond the object, Thames & Hudson, London, 1988

Williams, Gareth, Branded?, V&A Publications, London, 2000

NOTES

All quotations in the text, unless otherwise stated, are based on interviews with the author.

1. Thackara, John & Jane, Stuart, 'New British Design', Thames & Hudson, London, 1987

2. York, Peter, unidentified source

3. 'Business Week', June 1990

4. Philips, 'Visions of the Future', exhibition catalogue, V&K Publishing, Blaricum, The Netherlands, 1996

5. Philips, Undated press release. Supplied to author

6. Moore, Geoffrey, Crossing the Chasm: marketing and selling technology products to mainstream customers, Capstone Publishing, New York, 1999

7. Various authors, 'The Cyber Elite', 'Time', November 1998, p.30

8. Carlton, Jim, Apple: the 'Inside Story of Intrigue', 'Egomania and Business Blunders', Century Business Books, USA, 1997, p.429

9. Redhead, David, 'Apple Bites Back', 'Design', Autumn 1998, p.39

10. Salomon, Gitta, in David Redhead, 'Apple Bites Back', 'Design', Autumn 1998, p.42

11. Southwell, Tim, 'The return of the Mac', 'The Face', March 2002, p.113

12. Gibney Jnr, Frank and Belinda Luscombe, 'The redesigning of America', 'Time', 26 June 2000, p.51

13. Exhibition caption, Designer of the Year, Design Museum, London, 1 March–29 June 2003

14. Allen, Ted, quoted in 'Esquire', December 2002, p.143

15. Quittner, Josh, 'Apple's new core', 'Time', 14 January 2002, p.49

16. Jobs, Steve, quoted in Josh Quittner, 'Apple's new core', 'Time', 14 January 2002, p.48

17. Redhead, David, 'Psion User', Autumn 1998

18. Butter, Andrea and Pogue, David, 'Piloting Palm: the Inside Story of Palm, Handspring and the Birth of the Billion Dollar Handheld Industry', John Wiley & Sons, New York, 2002, p.204

19. Birch, Dave, 'Second Sight,' 'Guardian Unlimited Online', 8 May 2003. http://www.guardian.co.uk/online

20. Nokia, Marketing document, unpublished, undated. Supplied to author

21. Plant, Sadie, On the mobile, Motorola promotional document, 2002

22. G2 Special Report, 'Guardian', 11 November 2002

23. Durman, Paul, 'Nokia bets on a mobile world', 'The Sunday Times': Business section, 22 June 2003, p.11

24. Steinbock, Dan, 'The Nokia Revolution', Amacom, New York, 2001, p.272

25. Sullivan, Richard, 'Ring leader', 'American Vogue', April 2000

26. Exon, Mike, 'The Ring Road', 'Design Week', 12 June 2003, p.18

27. James Harkin, 'Mobilisation: the growing public interest in mobile technology', report published by Demos, London, June 2003

INDEX